CW00348961

# The Rise of Women in Higher Education

# The Rise of Women in Higher Education

## *How, Why, and What's Next*

Gary A. Berg

ROWMAN & LITTLEFIELD
Lanham • Boulder • New York • London

Published by Rowman & Littlefield
An imprint of The Rowman & Littlefield Publishing Group, Inc.
4501 Forbes Boulevard, Suite 200, Lanham, Maryland 20706
www.rowman.com

6 Tinworth Street, London SE11 5AL

Copyright © 2020 by Gary A. Berg

*All rights reserved.* No part of this book may be reproduced in any form or by any
electronic or mechanical means, including information storage and retrieval systems,
without written permission from the publisher, except by a reviewer who may quote
passages in a review.

British Library Cataloguing in Publication Information Available

**Library of Congress Cataloging-in-Publication Data**

Names: Berg, Gary A., 1955- author.
Title: The rise of women in higher education : how, why, and what's next / Gary A Berg.
Description: Lanham : Rowman & Littlefield, [2020] | Includes bibliographical references and index.
   | Summary: "Today women are outperforming men in college attendance and academic achieve-
   ment. Clearly, celebration for the tasks surmounted globally in opening broader access to higher
   education is called for, yet challenges remain, ones that are somewhat different than those
   apparent from the past. It's time to consider what this momentous change means for higher
   education and society. What forces are at play? What are the implications for higher education
   when women are a significant majority of students overall?"—Provided by publisher.
Identifiers: LCCN 2019039636 (print) | LCCN 2019039637 (ebook) | ISBN 9781475853612 (cloth) |
   ISBN 9781475853629 (paperback) | ISBN 9781475853636 (epub)
Subjects: LCSH: Women in higher education. | Academic achievement.
Classification: LCC LC1567 .B47 2020 (print) | LCC LC1567 (ebook) | DDC 378.0082—dc23
LC record available at https://lccn.loc.gov/2019039636
LC ebook record available at https://lccn.loc.gov/2019039637

♾ ™ The paper used in this publication meets the minimum requirements of American
National Standard for Information Sciences Permanence of Paper for Printed Library
Materials, ANSI/NISO Z39.48-1992.

To Leona, Linda, and Laura,
three generations of inspiring women

# Contents

# Acknowledgments

I need to first acknowledge Sarah Jubar, my acquisitions editor at Rowman & Littlefield, for recognizing and supporting this book project in the proposal form and through the production phase.

For the extensive research done in this book I relied heavily on the excellent UCLA library, and the network of libraries in the City of Los Angeles. Additionally, I used the resources of the Claremont Colleges. A special thank you to the Ella Strong Denison Library at Scripps College for access to their special collections.

Photos throughout the book are drawn from the Library of Congress collection.

I want to thank those former female colleagues who provided their insights on this important topic. Their unattributed quotes are used throughout the book.

Finally, as always, I am indebted to Dr. Linda Venis for her expert editing, wise counsel, and perspective.

# Author's Note

While there are certainly many photos of women marching and directly advocating for rights, the cover image ("Gathering Fruit," 1895, Cassatt, Mary, 1844–1926, artist, Library of Congress) evokes the way women together over time effectively collected knowledge informally and shared and cultivated it for generations.

# Introduction

## *The Rise of Women in Post-Secondary Education*

As a student and a college employee at five different universities for 50 years, I have been around higher education in America at a transformative moment in history. From a non-scientific, personal point of view, I first started to become aware of the change in the student body while working as a dean and associate vice president at California State University Channel Islands, the newest public university in the state. From the institution's modest beginnings to the present day, the campus slowly gained the confidence of the local community who began to send their daughters to attend in large numbers, especially young Latinas.

Additionally, the university welcomed a large number of dynamic female faculty members and administrators who as a group created an atmosphere different from what I had previously experienced. Then there were the female students—confident, serious, and dedicated to their studies and futures for themselves and their families.

Women are outpacing men in college attendance and performance. The trend has occurred slowly over time, but in fall 2017, 56.4% of those enrolled in all undergraduate programs in America were women. At non-degree granting institutions attendance by women is a stunning 69% (U.S. Department of Education, 2017). Graduation rates tell a compelling story of the educational success of women: 57.2% of the bachelor degrees in 2015–2016 were earned by women, and 59.2% of the master degrees. This pattern is also apparent at the doctoral level where women received 52.7% of the doctoral degrees—an important statistic because of the impact on the development of future faculty members.

On the college level, the change in the composition of universities is evident. In fall 2017 there were 1,236 degree-granting institutions that were 60% or more female, including 57 research institutions; 1,034 degree-granting institutions had 70% or more female students, and 566 were comprised of over 80% women (U.S. Department of Education, 2018).

This is not just an American phenomenon. On the international scene, female participation in higher education overall has increased and currently surpasses that of males in almost all developed countries. Since 1990, the global participation of women has increased at a faster rate than that of men, resulting after the turn of the century in tertiary enrollment parity (United Nations Statistics Division, 2015). Furthermore, results from a global reading assessment showed that girls outperformed boys in every participating country (a margin roughly equivalent to one year of schooling). Girls also appear to be narrowing the gaps in achievement in mathematics where boys have historically held an advantage (OECD, 2014).

Eggins (1997) contends that the last decades of the 20th century and first decades of the 21st century tell a remarkable story of the expanding role for women in society, especially in leadership roles in organizations, including notably higher education. There is some indication internationally of a general awareness of the need to continue increased participation and leadership for women in multiple sectors of society, especially in providing educational quality, as well as leadership in government.

Almost two-thirds of the people around the world, including men, feel that the world would be a better place if men thought like women (Gerzema & D'Antonio, 2013). Sixty-five percent believe that more female leadership in government would prompt a rise in trust and fairness, and a decline in war and scandal. According to Gerzema and D'Antonio's book, *The Athena Doctrine,* based on extensive international surveys, there is a recognition not only of the need for more women in leadership positions, but for men to adopt female mindsets.

> Powered by cooperation, communication, nurturing and inclusiveness, among others, institutions, businesses, and individuals are breaking from old masculine structures and mindsets to become more flexible, collaborative, and caring. Our data show that this change is deemed necessary, and is welcomed, by strong majorities in every country we surveyed. (p. 255)

The evidence of successful leadership by women is mounting. Financial funds run by women outperform those run by men. Shares of large companies with women board members outperformed comparable companies with all-male boards by 26% (Gerzema & D'Antonio, 2013).

Today, women are outperforming men generally in college attendance and academic achievement, but there is a recognition of challenges and uneven progress in educating women worldwide. Clearly, celebration for the distance traveled nationally and internationally in opening broader access to higher education is called for, yet tasks remain, ones that are somewhat different than those of the past. For universities the test for the future is to make needed changes in broad areas within higher education from financial aid to curriculum, student activities, and overall campus culture to better foster a newly empowered majority of women students.

It's time to consider what this momentous change means for higher education and society. What forces are at play? What are the implications for higher education when women are a significant majority of students overall?

## ORGANIZATION OF THE BOOK

The overall concentration of this book is on the global social-political context for the rise of women in higher education, specific public policies such as the important Title IX legislation in America, and the role of informal learning in the historical evolution. The large areas of discussion on the woman suffrage and feminist movements, which are deeply covered elsewhere, are only touched on here.

The book's first chapter looks at the history and social context of women in higher education. Statistics on changes in student participation, faculty, and university administration composition are considered. The history of resistance to women entering the academy is traced by exploring the various types of institutions that arose in the late 19th century, including men-only, women-only, coordinate, and coeducational institutions.

The specific trend of the increase of female faculty members and university administrators is measured, with a focus on the lack of parity between men and women in compensation, rank, academic discipline, and where they work. The encouraging pattern of increased participation is tempered by remaining inequalities in compensation, as well as restricted employment in prestigious disciplines and colleges. Finally, the disturbing issue of student debt is observed, showing a greater average obligation for female students subsequent to graduation, a result partly of earning on average 80% of that earned by males.

In Chapter 2, the larger international environment of the tertiary education of women is detailed, along with a discussion of its literacy and economic development facets. While by the year 2000 women equaled men in participation in higher education, large disparities still exist in participation in the important fields of Science, Technology, Engineering and Mathematics (STEM). The link between reduced child birth and increased higher education is considered, as well as the changing legal and political environments for women around the globe. Data on comparative gender skills worldwide and possible causes are analyzed, challenging assumptions about innate differences between males and females. The chapter ends by observing the increased leadership roles for women in public office, and the connection between the education of women and economic development.

In Chapter 3, the contentious development of women's and coeducational colleges in the 19th and early 20th centuries is outlined. The history of the women's college movement, which developed in response to exclusion from men's institutions, is sketched, along with a discussion of the unique differences in purposes and strategies of these schools. The rapid growth of coeducational institutions following the Civil War, pushed along by growing women's social activism and a need for classroom teachers, is described. In order to gain an appreciation of the uniqueness of colleges for women, specific institutions are presented, including Xavier University of Louisiana (HBCU, Catholic, women's), The New School (predominantly women, continuing education), Mount Saint Mary's University (Catholic, women's), and Scripps College (second wave women's college).

Chapter 4 turns to the all-important Title IX legislation in America and the consequent impact on both women's sports and university culture. The complex historical context of women's athletics, as well as data revealing the impact of Title IX legislation on the rapid growth of collegiate women's athletics at the end of the 20th century, is reported. The divergent histories of women and men's athletics is documented, showing women's closer ties to academic departments, and females in sports academically outperforming males. The chapter ends with a discussion of perspectives on the media representation of women athletes.

Chapter 5 reflects on how women in America and Europe developed literacy through informal ways of acquiring knowledge that prepared them for successful entry into the academy. The importance of alternative ways of women's learning and expressing themselves through writing and reading in the late 18th and 19th centuries is investigated. In particular, the 19th century women's novels that dominated England and America, as well as aspects of informal learning practices such as reading circles and continuing education groups like the Chautauqua Movement, are explored in this chapter. College fiction and film in America are analyzed to better understand these evolving vehicles for women writers, as well as the depiction of women in popular media. This chapter presents an often-overlooked aspect of women in higher education that helps to explain why women were so successful in college once restrictions were slowly lifted—advantages in literacy that continue today.

Chapter 6 explores late 20th-century approaches to the advanced education of women that came about in conjunction with the Civil Rights and Feminist Movements of the 1960s and 1970s. By the 1980s, Women's Studies programs became common in American universities but were beset with ongoing internal debates about the wisdom of creating bifurcated academic departments as opposed to incorporating new viewpoints within existing curricula. Feminist pedagogy arose at the same time with the idea that women's ways of knowing and learning were not honored in the traditional university. The chapter considers contemporary viewpoints on how Women's or Gender Studies, as well as feminist pedagogy, are viewed in the academy today.

The book concludes with an appreciation for the complexity of the social history of gender and education, and a belief that understanding the particulars is important and necessary to moving forward.

## THEMES IN THE BOOK

The reader would benefit by keeping in mind the following themes in apprising what follows:

- The gender gap in education in relation to labor and compensation

    While the statistics on the participation of women in higher education internationally is certainly positive, disparity in annual income persists. It is important to grasp the impact of gendered disciplines, childbirth and family care, and cultural attitudes.
- Financial Aid debt for women

    Women on average leave college with greater debt that men, and combined with lower average income, the long-term impact may be reduced interest of women in college. Or, will a more critical perspective by female students on potential careers lead to different occupations?
- The important link between birthrates and the education of women

    Historically, countries around the world experienced increases in the education of women as birthrates declined over time. This pattern is connected to economic modernization, changing cultural values, and the availability of birth control. Nevertheless, childcare continues to impact both female students and faculty members.
- International higher education and economic development

    Women and poverty internationally are strongly associated. The sad fact is that most of those who live in a state of poverty are women and children. Advanced tertiary education for women can provide a significant increase in a nation's workforce, and break the cyclical pattern of poverty.
- Women's athletics and changing college culture

    The shift in focus for colleges from primarily male athletics to the inclusion of women's sports has enlarged the overall campus environment. Women's athletics provide a balanced approach to college sports with a focus on human development and academic achievement, and may be a model for the future. Similarly, women more actively participate in student activities and leadership than ever before.

- The tenure system and the slow progress toward equity for female faculty members

    Although women are now equally represented generally in higher education, they are disproportionately represented in two-year community colleges and at less prestigious four-year institutions. The faculty search, promotion, and tenure system so prevalent in American higher education may be slowing progress for women faculty members. More rigid standards for reviewing the academic work of female scholars, and for some, a less sympathetic attitude toward family responsibilities, may disadvantage women faculty.

- The complexity of female identities

    Rather than thinking about women as one group, it is important to appreciate the intersection of race, socio-economic status, and age.

- Learning from women's colleges

    While there are fewer and fewer women-only colleges, there are still important things that may be learned from these institutions such as providing role models in female faculty and administration, establishing a professional network, and giving an opportunity for women to study in all fields.

- Learning outside the classroom

    The history of women reveals that faced with a society intent on limiting women's opportunities for advanced education, they turned to reading, writing, reading groups, and continuing education. Might informal learning continue to be important for women, whether it is through simply reading, continuing education, or forms of distance learning?

- Self-confidence and female students

    Women outstudy and outperform men in academic achievement, but rate themselves lower on every intellectual scale. Self-assurance in higher education is especially important for many women. The context for the development of self-confidence is complex, involving family relationships, gender norms and expectations, and personal experience.

With these themes in mind, I invite the reader in what follows to engage in the momentous story of the rise of women in higher education.

*Chapter One*

# Participation of Women in Higher Education

In this chapter we engage directly with the primary topic of the book—the increase in women students, faculty members, and administration in post-secondary education. The story begins with the initial restriction of women, follows their gradual involvement through separate women's institutions, coordinate colleges, and eventual blending with male students in coeducational colleges. The tale includes the post–World War II proportional decline of women in higher education, the slow rise of female enrollment at the end of the 20th century, and the various forms of resistance women encountered over time.

Finally, in order to balance the positive news of women's increased access to higher education, we analyze the statistics on women in higher administration, including comparative compensation levels. While numerical increases in women generally are clear, a deeper look at the numbers exposes continuing disparity in rank, prestige, and compensation. The chapter ends by considering the disturbing statistics on student debt in America, which is especially large for female graduates and may foretell of negative imminent consequences.

## HISTORICAL PERSPECTIVE

The origin of women's education and institutions in America began in the Revolutionary War period when a new appreciation of the value of women and their labor in early colonial society arose. Politically, they were as a group bearers of the new culture, the Mothers of the Republic, and needed educating. Early American history saw women playing the crucial role of the

**Figure 1.1.   Nine African American women, full-length portrait, seated on steps of a building at Atlanta University, Georgia (1899). *Askew, Thomas E., photographer (Library of Congress).***

guarantor of civic virtue, a role combining political and educational obliga-tion (Faragher, 1988). Some prominent women during the revolution, such as Abigail Adams, insisted that the new society created by the American Revo-lution should make room for educated women, although most at the time failed to see a place for women in college (Solomon, 1985).

During the first one and a half centuries in the early history of America, little serious thought was given to the education of women at the advanced level. College education was primarily for specific professions such as the clergy and law, and these were exclusively men's occupations. As a result, there was no apparent need or desire to include women in college.

Women in early America were pushed into significant home responsibil-ities because of a limited overall workforce and the lack of a servant class found in Europe. As a result, home or domestic studies became an important part of the education of women. In colonial America, marriage was the chief means of livelihood for most women. American women married earlier than European women, typically between 20 and 23, and understood their primary duty was to bear children who could help with family farm labor, and there-fore would have less time for formal education (Rudolph, 1990; Solomon, 1985).

"Academies" and "seminaries" were formed to educate women for the republic, and accomplish religious and civic work. "Academy" usually indi-cated that it was a young men's primary or secondary school. "Seminary" was the name given to colleges. Harvard, for instance, called itself a "semi-nary" (Boas, 1935). In the early 19th century, women's seminaries offered a slightly less rigorous college curriculum than that available to men.

Women could contribute to society by teaching the young in formal set-tings (Turpin, 2016). Four of these pre-college institutions had special impor-tance and influence: Emma Willard's in Troy, New York (1821), Catharine Beecher's in Hartford, Connecticut (1828), Zilpah Grant's in Ipswich, Mas-sachusetts (1828), and Mary Lyon's in South Hadley, Massachusetts (1837) (Horowitz, 1984). By the early and mid-19th century leaders urging women's education emerged such as Lyon, Beecher, and Benjamin Rush (Woody, 1929).

A "normal school" is the terminology for an institution created to train high school graduates to become teachers by educating them in pedagogical and curricular norms of the time. Often normal schools are overlooked in the history of women's education, but they did provide access for females to advanced education with a focus on teacher training and writing. Many wom-en's colleges started as women-only normal schools. Ritter (2012) claims that the level of the teaching of writing at the normal schools was surprising-ly high, on a level with the elite institutions of the time. Although women's colleges were socially conservative, they were often educationally progres-sive by redefining writing and literacy in artistic and creative terms.

Most institutions were church-founded or affiliated up until the Civil War, and their leadership was in the hands of the clergy; indeed, nine of ten college presidents were appointed from the church. The pre–Civil War wom-en's educational institutions were mostly church-sponsored and not equal to men's colleges in the quality or the level of their curricula (Newcomer, 1959).

As educating children became a more common occurrence, the need for classroom teachers grew, which was exacerbated by the Civil War. Men made two to four times as much as women as teachers, and one clear reason for the increase of women teachers was the fact that they were cheaper. By 1870 three out of five teachers nationally were women (Newcomer, 1959).

Furthermore, with a surplus of women after the Civil War, seminaries became a more acceptable option for women, as it was statically less likely that they would marry. By midcentury men could not argue against the possibility or practicality of women learning, only its propriety (Boas, 1935). Soon the public saw the practical advantage of educating women who would become classroom teachers: "they began to have their doubts as to the wisdom of half-educating them" (Boas, 1935, p. 81).

Teaching and writing were the two most acceptable occupations outside the home for women in the 19th century, and writing paid at a higher rate (see Chapter 5). Women writers of the time were at first often anonymous—typically women completely omitted their names from the title pages of their books, or used just a single letter to represent themselves. Women teachers were more visible, and employed broadly because they were economical.

Women entered into the academy in the mid-19th century because of both the practical need for classroom teachers and the evolving human rights discussions paralleling the end of slavery. The industrial age and the improving American economy led to more leisure time for American women—hence, an increased focus on education as well as charity work. Women's rights issues had taken a back seat to charity work in the early 19th century because of a focus instead on the abolition of slavery (Boas, 1935). Additionally, educating women to be teachers became a respected practice by religious groups seeking to Christianize the frontier (Solomon, 1985).

The education of women in America diverged from European traditions because of both practical and cultural differences in the New World. Mary Wollstonecraft's (see Chapter 5) early feminist influence in England did not extend to America, where duties instead of rights were often emphasized. Nevertheless, there was clear interest by American women in acquiring formal education at all levels.

For instance, in 1826 in Boston, a public high school was opened for girls, and was overrun with interest from the local citizens. Nevertheless, it closed after two years because of consistent complaints and the unwillingness of male taxpayers to use public money to fund the education of women (Boas, 1935). In the South there were some colleges awarding women degrees, but this was looked on with suspicion in the North (Boas, 1935). In general, these early women's colleges were considered of low quality compared to men's institutions.

College was almost exclusively the world of white men until the mid-19th century when two additional options led to the increased entrance of women into the academy: the development of women's colleges, and the rise of coeducational colleges (covered in detail in Chapter 3). It would be two hundred and one years after Harvard College opened until American women received a college degree equal to men when four women enrolled at Oberlin College, and three received baccalaureate degrees in 1841 (Newcomer, 1959). It wasn't until 1849 that the first woman earned a degree in medicine, and 1869 when the first female lawyer was qualified (Boas, 1935). At the same time, the end of the 19th century showed slow progress in the legal position of women in gaining rights to property and divorce (Boas, 1935).

By 1910 men and women attended college in almost equal numbers, but because many women enrolled in two-year teacher's training programs, they were behind in the ratio of bachelor's degrees (Figure 1.2).

It is important to note that, contrary to some impressions, the early period of gender parity in college enrollments from 1900 to 1930 (which recurs at the end of the 20th century) was not the result of only women from wealthy families attending women's colleges in greater numbers, but a broad trend in American society.

The college gender gap began to widen in favor of men during the Depression Era because of high unemployment and the desire to enhance employability (Goldin, Katz, & Kuziemko, 2006). Following World War II, the GI Bill financed college education for men who had fought for America, and caused historic change in the demographics of higher education, creating a far more diverse group of students. College expanded across the ranks of American social classes and increasingly became a job entry requirement.

The relative advance for women in both college graduation and attendance rates began in the 1950s, but was especially rapid for the generation born in the late 1940s. Parity was reached by those born in the 1960s, and the female attendance advantage widened considerably in the following decade. For groups born around 1950, the relative graduation rate was equal to that realized earlier in the century for cohorts born from 1880 to 1910.

In sum, the return to the previous level of participation by women took almost four decades. Great demographic change occurred from the late 1960s to the mid-1970s which impacted the statistics on college going; most importantly the age of marriage began a rapid ascent. The median age of marriage among female college graduates increased by 2.6 years, from 22.4 to 25 years old (Goldin, Katz, & Kuziemko, 2006).

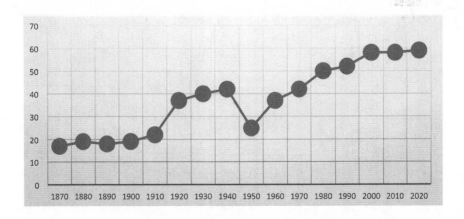

Figure 1.2. Percentage of U.S. Bachelor Degrees Awarded to Women. *NCES.*

Labor force participation for women also increased greatly: 49% were employed in 1970 at ages 30 to 34, while ten years later, 70% were employed. One crucial factor was access to reliable contraception through birth control pills which positively impacted women's college going and graduation. Rising career expectations for women also led to better preparation for college.

The largest narrowing in the gender gap in high school math and science course enrollment occurred between 1972 and 1982. Better preparation eventually paid off as girls improved greatly in math and reading test scores relative to boys, from 1980 to 1992. Not only did girls advance to college at greater rates, eventually at rates exceeding those of boys, but they also began to take courses and major in fields that were more career-oriented rather than the previous emphasis on the humanities (Goldin, Katz & Kuziemko, 2006).

Once barriers to female careers were lowered and their access to higher education was expanded, two key factors may have played a role in the female college advantage: relatively greater economic benefits of college for females, and conversely, higher effort costs of college going and preparation for males. According to most estimates, the wage premium of attending college is actually higher for women than men (Dougherty, 2005). Also, the rise in divorce rates since the 1960s, and women's greater economic responsibility for children, created incentives for women to invest in higher education.

In the seminal article "The Homecoming of American College Women: The Reversal of the College Gender Gap," (Goldin, Katz & Kuziemko, 2006) the authors argued that the widened job-market prospects in the 1970s led more women to compete directly with men in secondary school and college, and increasingly surpass them. Beginning in the late 1960s and early 1970s, young women's expectations of their future labor force participation radically changed, and their college-enrollment and graduation rates relative to males began to soar. This group of baby boomers changed behavior by taking more math and science courses in high school, choosing different college majors, marrying and having children later, and demonstrating focus on their own careers.

The enrollment pattern gradually changed over the ending decades of the 20th century as women proportionally overtook men. Since fall 1988, the number of female students in postbaccalaureate programs in America has exceeded the number of male students, and has been gradually increasing. Between 2005 and 2015, the number of full-time male postbaccalaureate students increased by 24%, compared with a 25% increase in the number of full-time female postbaccalaureate students. Among part-time postbaccalaureate students, the number of males enrolled in 2015 was 6% higher than in 2005, while the number of females was eight percent higher (U.S. Department of Education, National Center for Education Statistics, 2018). The most recent figures show that 56.4% of enrolled four-year students are women, and 56.5% at two-year institutions. At non-degree granting institutions women surpass men at a rate of 69% (U.S. Department of Education, 2017).

In addition to enrollment numbers, graduation rates give a strong indication of gender trends (Figure 1.3). In the most recent data from the Department of Education, women are out achieving men in graduation rates: 57.2% of bachelor degrees in 2015-16 were earned by women; 59.2% master degrees; and 52.7% doctoral degrees (U.S. Department of Education, 2017).

Since 1979 more women than men have been in college, and as of the year 2000 more women ages 25 to 29 have completed college than men (U.S. Census Bureau, 2000). The Department of Education estimates that by the year 2026 the national student body will be comprised of 57% women (Marcus, 2017). Importantly, because of the implications for the development of future faculty members, this trend is also apparent at the doctoral level. In 2002 for the first time in history, more American women than men received doctorates from American universities (Hoffer et al., 2009).

From the institutional point of view, in America in fall 2017 there were 1,236 degree granting institutions with 60% or more female students, including 57 research institutions. 1,034 degree granting institutions with 70% or more female students, and 566 degree granting institutions with over 80% women (NCES, IPEDS, 2018).

However, even though women's average (self-reported) grades in high school are better, a larger percentage of women than men enroll in college, and a higher percentage graduate from four-year colleges, they still trail considerably in financial rewards within six years of graduation. Additional-

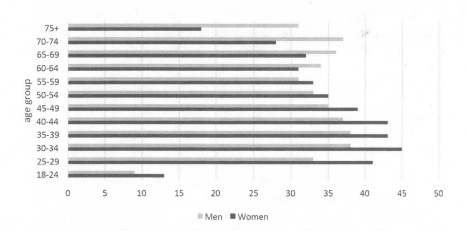

**Figure 1.3.    College Degree Gender Gap by Age.** *U.S. Census (Percent Bachelor Degree or Higher 2018).*

ly, more women than men borrow money to attend college, and because women's incomes after earning degrees are, on average, far lower than men's, they are left with a disproportionately high level of debt (*Chronicle of Higher Education*, 2018).

One important aspect of the participation trend is the variance by ethnicity. While college enrollment rates among young people in general have risen in recent decades, a Pew Research Center analysis of U.S. Census Bureau data show that females outpace males in college enrollment, especially among Hispanics and African Americans (Lopez & Gonzales-Barrera, 2014). In 1994, among Hispanics who completed high school, about half of both men and women immediately enrolled in college. Nearly two decades later, college enrollments for both groups improved, but women outpaced men by 13 percentage points.

For African American high school graduates, it's a different story. In 1994, young black male high school graduates were more likely than their female counterparts to enroll in college. By 2012, the pattern had reversed. The share of young African American men enrolled in college remained stagnant, while the share of young black women enrolled in college increased to 69%—a 12% point gap with black men.

It's worth noting that the backdrop to these shifts is the changing demographics of the nation's public-school student population. In 1994, Hispanics made up 14% of public-school students, African Americans 17%, Asian Americans and Native Americans 4%, and whites 65%. By 2012, 25% of all public-school students were Hispanic while 16% were African American, 8% Asian American or Native American and 51% white, demonstrating the growing influence of the nation's non-white students (Lopez & Gonzales-Barrera, 2014).

The gender gap in college enrollment is not limited to Hispanic and African American youth. In 1994, among high school graduates, 62% of young white men and 66% of young white women were enrolled in college immediately after graduation—a 4% point gender gap. In 2012, that gap had grown to 10% points as the share of young white women enrolled in college grew to 72% while the rate for men remained the same (Lopez & Gonzales-Barrera, 2014). Among Asian Americans, there's been a less dramatic shift. Among them, the share of high school graduates going to college immediately after graduation also grew during this time period for both young men and women, but the gap is much smaller than that among other groups.

However, Goldin, Katz and Kuziemko (2006) contend that the decline in the male-to-female ratio of undergraduates during the past 35 years is neither due to changes in the ethnic mix of the college-aged population, nor to the types of postsecondary institutions they attend. Instead, the reduction in the ratio of male-to-female undergraduates never changes based on a range of factors (full-time and part-time enrollment, ethnic groups, etc.) and is apparent for all types of institutions.

Nevertheless, the female advantage in college enrollment and graduation is now substantially larger for Hispanics and African Americans than for whites. The new gender gap favoring females is found throughout the socioeconomic status distribution, with little variation. In contrast to the traditional pattern, the female advantage has become greatest for the children of families with low socioeconomic status.

Many scholars have offered reasons for the widening gender gap in educational participation and attainment. Some have pointed to economic factors—as labor market barriers to women have been lowered, the benefits of a college education grew more for women than men. According to Goldin, Katz and Kuziemko (2006), two transformations since World War II greatly increased the financial return to women's higher education: an increase in female life-cycle labor force participation, and a large shift in female employment into many previously male-dominated jobs, combined with a further increase in female labor force participation.

Additionally, the higher incidence of behavioral and school disciplinary problems among boys may be a factor in declining proportional college participation. Klevan, Weinberg and Middleton (2016) used data from the 2002 Educational Longitudinal Study to examine social capital and quantify the strength of its relationship to college enrollment, showing that men are disadvantaged with respect to key social capital variables. Other scholars argue that the higher incidence of behavioral problems among boys, and poorer study habits, lead to worse school performance (Goldin, Katz, & Kuziemko, 2006).

Boys have a much higher incidence than do girls of school disciplinary and behavior problems, and spend far fewer hours doing homework (Jacob, 2002). They also have two to three times the rate of Attention Deficit Hyperactivity Disorder (ADHD) than girls and much higher rates of criminal activity (Cuffe, Moore, & McKeown, 2003; Federal Bureau of Investigation, 2004). Furthermore, boys are also much more likely than girls to be placed in special education programs.

A record 25% of husbands are now married to wives who have more education than they do. This has reversed a long-term trend since the 1960s when it was much more common for a husband to have more education than his wife. The shift happened mostly after 1990 when the share of husbands who were better educated than their wives started to fall. During the same period, young women surpassed men in college enrollment and graduation rates (Wang, 2017).

When asked about qualities in a potential spouse or partner, never-married men place more importance on choosing someone who shares their ideas about raising a family, while never-married women view having a steady job and financial security as a top priority in a potential partner. Therefore, even when women "marry down" educationally, they continue to "marry up" in income because men continue to outearn women, despite having less education overall. Wang (2017) notes three reasons for this earnings differential: sexism, uneven family responsibilities, and employment in different fields.

## RESISTANCE TO WOMEN IN COLLEGE

Change in social expectations for women were slow in coming during the 19th century. Opposition to women in college is epitomized by Edward Clarke's *Sex in Education* (1873) in which the Harvard Medical School professor contended that women students, for purely biological reasons, risked using up their limited energy studying, and would endanger their female organs:

> That undue and disproportionate brain activity exerts a sterilizing influence upon both sexes is alike a doctrine of physiology, and an induction from experience. And both physiology and experience also teach that this influence is more potent upon the female than upon the male. (Clarke, 1873, p. 137)

Despite the lower childbirth rates and the improved economic position of families, some obstructionists continued to argue that it was best for American society for women to focus on families rather than college (Solomon, 1985).

Part of the resistance to women in college was rooted in practical economic realities. Men were more encouraged to go to college because of traditions established in affluent families, and the greater expected financial return for men over women given unequal access to careers and high salaries. Women, on the other hand, still had the primary responsibility for child rearing and were anticipated to require breaks in their work lives outside the home for that reason. Newcomer (1959), expressing the public thinking of that time in considering statistics which seem to show less interest in college by women, noted,

> How many are concerned over the waste of our national resources when they are told that among the top 10 percent of our high school seniors the proportion of girls with no plans for going to college is more than double that for boys? Is the higher education of women wasted, or is it a waste not to educate more of the ablest young women than we do? (p. 246)

However, what Newcomer did not know writing at the end of the 1950s was that participation by women in college was about to change dramatically in America during the period of immense social change coming at the end of the 20th century.

**Figure 1.4.** *The Sky is Now Her Limit* (1920). *Illustration by Bushnell, reprinted in* New York Times Current History *(Library of Congress).*

The success of coeducation which became dominant in the 20th century induced a strong counter-reaction from some sectors of the population. Academic achievement was sometimes held against females when they surpassed males, and many faculty members supported the views of insecure students who charged that women interfered with the academic performance of men. The general critical argument was that female students either drove men out of the classroom by causing the discipline to be watered down, or were a distraction.

In terms of majors and university planning, the fear was that unless men enrolled in a program in substantial numbers, the subject of study was "feminized" and therefore not valuable career-wise. Yet the practical reality was that women could find employment most easily in teaching and thus focused on liberal arts courses, whereas men had access to more varied employment options and could study in a large range of disciplines (Solomon, 1985). In this way, academic disciplines were gendered from the start.

As a reaction to the perceived negative feminization of the university, admission restrictions were put in place (Gordon, 1990). For instance, between 1902 and 1915 Wesleyan College banned women students altogether, while the University of Rochester, Tufts University, and Western Reserve University set up women's coordinate colleges (separate from male students). The opening of the University of Chicago was a landmark in the progress of coeducation with women recruited as undergraduates, graduates, and faculty members. However, its success caused a counter-reaction when women not only attended in great numbers but also began to outperform men—evidenced by the fact that in 1902, 56.3% of Phi Beta Kappa students in the college were women.

Subsequently, this innovative university debated the question of women's admissions policies and decided to establish separate gender-based classes for freshmen and sophomore students. Similarly, Stanford was also, from the beginning, a place intended to be open to women. But when the attendance of women soared and they outperformed men academically, Stanford's leadership implemented a policy in 1904 restricting admissions to only one for every three men, a policy not overturned until 1933 (Solomon, 1985).

Some university administrators refused to give in to uncertainties of the feminization of college. When at the University of California (UC) attendance by women increased from 9% in 1870 to 46% in 1900, many male students and faculty feared that women were driving men out of the university and argued for segregated classes, but officials refused to restrict the admission of women. As a result, male enrollment did subsequently decline at Berkeley, especially in the humanities.

Some of the policies established during this time period to restrict enrollment by women remained in place all the way up until the 1960s. In the early 20th century educators were disturbed not only by the large numbers of women going to college, but also rising ethnic diversity, leading to racial caps on admissions, especially Jews. In this way the restrictions on women admissions were consistent with those placed on other outsider groups. Distressingly, some women's colleges at the time also limited Jewish students (Solomon, 1985).

During WWI the proportion of women in college increased from 43% to 53% nationally. After World War II, the GI Bill interrupted the proportional increase of women in college with a significant public policy shift (Solomon, 1985). This was followed in the 1950s by resistance to women on campus growing harsher with a general social shift to political conservatism (Gordon, 1990).

One very revealing publication in 1975 from the College Entrance Examination Board entitled *I Can Be Anything: Careers and Colleges for Young Women* (Mitchell, 1975) with a foreword by Anne Pride, president of the feminist publishing company KNOW, gives a sense of the struggles of women that persisted into the later part of the 20th century.

> This book clearly demonstrates that you cannot be free to choose if in your mind the options are narrowed only to the future life style of being a wife to a husband who makes all the decisions. In order to make a real choice there must be a possibility for you to choose to go to college, to go to graduate school, to have children, to raise children, to move anywhere, to accept a promotion, to go anywhere for a training program, to have a home of your own or to share with another. (Mitchell, 1975, p. xiii)

The book points out specific statistics of the period: nine out of 10 women working at some point in their lives; 19% widowed, divorced, or separated; and 23% single working women. Furthermore, the volume encourages women to look at non-traditional careers, arguing, "Does it make sense to you that the skills and talents of half of the population should be used mostly in a handful of occupations, like nurse, secretary, teacher?" (Mitchell, 1975, p. 2).

This practical guide profiles various careers including engineering, wherein a female engineer is interviewed and states: "I don't want my day to discourage the future engineer. If you want to carry on two jobs full time, engineer and homemaker, then the work days become very long. If you love both jobs the length of the day is all pleasure" (Mitchell, 1975, p. 90). Additionally, the author lists the number of women in engineering at specific colleges. For instance, at UC Berkeley at the time, only eight women, out of 490 total students, were enrolled in the engineering major.

## FEMALE FACULTY INCREASES AND COMPENSATION

As a result of their influence, perspective, and visibility, one area to assess in the growth of women in higher education is the percentage of women in the ranks of the faculty. As shown in Figure 1.5, the number of female faculty members in America steadily increased in overall percentage at the end of the 20th century, and then reached 49.3% in 2016, up from 41.72% in 2010, 41.38% in 2000, and 33.2% in 1987 (U.S. Department of Education, 2017).

Nevertheless, women faculty remain underrepresented in many disciplines and institutions in the United States (Reinert, 2016). Furthermore, there is clear evidence that a pay gap persists amongst men and women (Roach, 2014). Many studies have examined various types of gender discrimination for faculty and two areas in particular are problematic—annual salaries, and representation of female faculty in the upper ranks of academia.

According to the American Association of University Professors (AAUP), women were paid on average 81.6% of what men were paid in 2018–19 academic year (Figure 1.6). The differences are attributable primarily to an unequal distribution of employment between men and women in terms of institution type and faculty rank. The large disparity was found especially in the representation of women in the rank of professor (AAUP, 2019).

One important factor in the comparative compensation calculation is the disproportionate percentage of female faculty in the lower-paying two-year institutions. As one can see from Figure 1.7, while female faculty full professors are clearly a minority in doctoral degree institutions, they are a slight majority in community colleges.

Lack of resources and high teaching loads at community colleges tend to impact scholarship production (Glazer-Raymo, 2008).

Specific studies, such as that by Marine and Aleman (2018), have focused on the generational dispositions of tenured women faculty regarding professional identity and career. O'Meara et al. (2017) found women faculty spend more time on campus service, student advising, and teaching-related activities, while men spend more time on research. Women received more and different kinds of new work requests than men. According to Glazer-Raymo

**Figure 1.5.    Women Faculty in U.S. *U.S. Dept. of Education.***

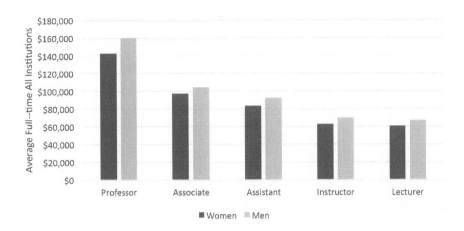

**Figure 1.6.  Comparative Faculty Compensation by Gender.** *AAUP, 2019.*

(2008), female faculty members are often unprepared for the large service requirement they have as faculty members.

In terms of overall job satisfaction, Webber and Rogers (2018) revealed a similarity between female and male faculty members in some aspects of work, but found differences in perceptions of department fit, recognition, work-life balance, and mentoring, which were more important to women faculty's satisfaction than for male peers.

Some scholars write that for women faculty navigation strategies are integral to succeeding in their careers within an environment that typically privileges men. Women faculty often utilize silence, consciously or subconsciously, as a tool to advance their careers. O'Meara et al. (2017) argue that women faculty use and experience silence daily in their academic careers to manage and negotiate identities, preserve their careers or selves, and to hide or conceal identities and emotions while conforming to cultural and institutional expectations. Women faculty often use an approach of "strategic silence," and purposefully use their voices in specific situations or contexts to push toward change or fight for a cause.

The American Economic Association in its Professional Climate Survey (2019) found that 48% of the female members surveyed felt they had been discriminated against on the basis of sex within the last 10 years; 20% said they'd been discriminated against due to marital status or caregiving responsibilities. Twenty-three percent of women said they had faced bias over their research topics, and 16% of women had faced it due to age.

As women have gained power and position in the academy, men have increased the privilege of commercial majors with more power (business, engineering). On the other hand, female faculty members who publish femi-

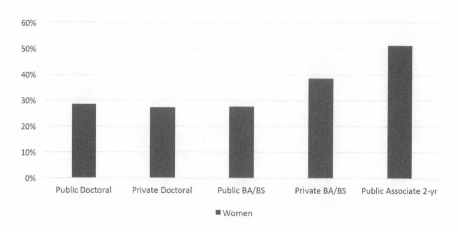

**Figure 1.7. Women Professors by Institutional Type** *AAUP, 2019.*

nist scholarship are often looked down upon (Glazer-Raymo, 2008). Research grant funding for scholarship is another important measure of faculty member success where disparity based on gender is apparent. In a study looking at National Institutes of Health grants from 2006 to 2017, female first-time principal investigators received a median grant of $126,615 across all grant and institution types during that period, while first-time male grantees were awarded $165,721 (Oliveira, Woodruff & Uzzi, 2019).

## ADMINISTRATIVE INCREASES AND COMPENSATION

The number of women in higher education administration is growing slowly, but still clearly unequal. The profile of a typical American university president continues to be a white male in his early 60s. Females constituted less than 5% of American college presidents in 1975 (Touchton, Shavlik, & Davis, 1993), and increased to 30% by 2016. Furthermore, the percentage of college presidents who were ethnic minorities was 17% in 2016 (American Council on Education, 2017).

Women are also less likely to hold the senior administrative positions of academic dean, executive vice president or provost that mostly commonly serve as pathways to the presidency, representing only 23% of provosts, 16% of executive vice presidents, and 19% of deans (King & Gomez, 2008). Adoption of widespread antidiscrimination laws and organizational policies have failed to close sufficiently the gender gap in leadership. Overall, the goal of encouraging women to enter the leadership pipeline has not been met (Ely, Ibarra, & Kolb, 2011).

Some note that part of the challenge lies in traditional notions of leadership which tend to be modeled on typically male dispositions (Astin & Leland, 1991; Kezar, Carducci, & Contreras-McGavin, 2006; Nidiffer, 2001). It was not until the decade of the 1970s that scholars first began to consider gender differences in leadership. The absence of gender-related discussion in the leadership literature prior to the 1970s also reflects women's invisibility in organizational leadership roles in American society (Ely, Ibarra, & Kolb, 2011).

Longman and Madsen (2014) argue that reasons for underrepresentation of women in senior level leadership roles across university sectors are complex and multifaceted. For example, they point out that women may be more interested in high-impact versus high-profile jobs. Additionally, women leaders tend to behave differently, often concerned with attention to democratic and participatory forms of decision making based on alternate personal values.

Scholars take somewhat varied approaches in focusing on either progress or remaining challenges for women in higher education leadership. For instance, Wheat and Hill (2016) studied women senior administrators at doctorate-granting universities and found that participants did not view their gender as a barrier to the attainment of their current positions. However, the leaders indicated that gender does impact management styles and the positioning of family responsibilities in their professional roles. Similarly, historical case studies that focus on specific role models, such as in Sartorius (2014), portray a leading dean of the University of Kansas who became a role model for early women university administrators.

On the other hand, some take a critical perspective to examine women's progress in higher education (Glazer-Raymo, 2001). Aisenberg and Harrington (1988) drew on more than 60 interviews to examine women's struggle to gain authority in the academic profession. Gouthro, Taber and Brazil (2018) assessed the possibilities and challenges of viewing universities as inclusive learning organizations, with a particular focus on women in academic faculty and leadership roles, arguing that underlying systemic structures that privilege male scholars need to be challenged through shifts in policies to address ongoing issues of gender inequality in higher education.

Women presidents report that they find it more difficult to connect with male donors, and are less likely to immerse themselves completely in the university role (Glazer-Raymo, 2008). In general, more research needs to be done to understand the complex factors that might impede women's attainment of senior administrative roles and presidencies at especially doctoral degree-granting universities (Madsen, 2012).

# STUDENT DEBT

Student debt is becoming a national crisis in America: 44 million borrowers in the United States hold approximately $1.46 trillion in student debt. Moreover, women have nearly two-thirds of the outstanding student debt in the United States—almost $929 billion as of early 2019. Figure 1.8 displays average debt by ethnicity and gender, showing higher levels for minority women.

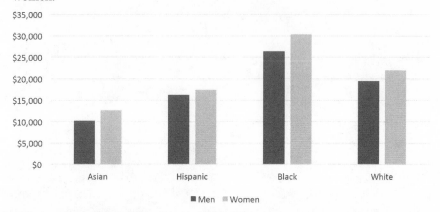

**Figure 1.8.   Average Debt BS/BA.** *AAUW, 2019.*

Women take about two years longer than men to repay student loans and are more likely to struggle economically as they do so. As a result, women often put off saving for retirement, buying a home, or starting a business. The situation is direr for African American and Hispanic women who pay off student loan debt even more slowly and experience more financial difficulties as they do so (Figure 1.9).

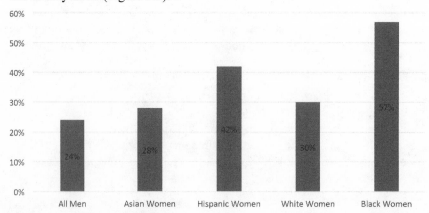

**Figure 1.9.   Difficulty Repaying Loans.** *AAUW, 2019.*

Women also take on larger student loans than do men, and because of the gender pay gap, they have less disposable income after graduation. This contributes to the fact that women take more time than men do in paying off debt.

The impact of this growing college debt, especially for women of color, is one of the most important statistics in this chapter. Clearly more needs to be done to understand the disparity in the debt amounts, and to determine how colleges can better serve students. In the long run the extreme debt load for individual female students is not sustainable, and the question for universities is to understand what they can do better to serve these students, lessen the debt, and increase subsequent wages.

## CONCLUSION

There is a growing public awareness of the rapid increase of women in college, as evidenced by the recent article entitled: "Girls Have Always Been Better at School. Now It Matters More: The higher-education gender gap has become a major factor in American political and economic life, and it yawns even wider in other rich countries" (Fox, 2019). Why are men now attending and graduating in post-secondary institutions at a lower rate? The answer to this important question is complex and not necessarily all good news for women.

Some factors to consider are that as undergraduate degrees have become more common, they are less unique and valuable. Second, majors have become increasingly important in a flooded academic degree environment and specialized workforce. Third, institutional reputation (ranking) has become more important, and thus we see the extreme lengths some parents go to try to win admission for their children. Fourth, men still may perceive more options in employment than women.

Perhaps a fundamental question is relevant here: How has the purpose of college changed so that women are now a majority? One thought is that the university has become increasingly a place of safe harbor for women. In a world of great complexity, uncertainty, and peril, with all their remaining problems, colleges are a place of relative safety and regulated fairness. This image of shelter is particularly important for first-generation female students with anxious parents. At the same time, the image of college as a male-dominated location for fraternities and the building of career networks for later life is becoming less common, and found mostly in elite institutions. In fact, one of the distinguishing differences remaining between public and private elite institutions is this very networking advantage.

The history of women's participation in college displays a long struggle to gain access as students, faculty, and administrators. Nevertheless, both in

America and globally, clear progress has been made to the point that women are surpassing men in participation, as well as in achievement. Challenges clearly remain in female student involvement in specific academic fields, women faculty in rank and compensation levels, and administrators at elite research institutions and in compensation parity.

One reason for the slowness to change in faculty compensation and rank may be the traditional tenure system. This strongly hierarchical system gives in many ways unchecked authority to those in place over entrance and advancement into the academy. Additionally, the level of compensation for faculty and university administrators mirrors the finding in society in general that females typically earn 80 percent on average of what males do.

It is also typical in looking at social change through education to talk about pipelines and the front-loading of qualified women needed to work themselves through the system. Certainly, the balanced number of women now graduating from doctoral programs bodes well for the future. Nevertheless, gendering of specific academic fields, so that women are disproportionately in the lower paid ones, clearly exacerbates the problem of unequal compensation in the academy and in society.

Female administrators and faculty members I surveyed for this book pointed to the differences in economic need which lead to men more often going to work after high school: "Young men are looking at and/or need immediate sources of decent income, so more difficult or not tempting to give up immediate income." Additionally, for some military service is another option: "Perhaps more go into military service because they think it is a safer route to employment."

One respondent pointed to the overall devaluing of degrees with a greater proportion of the population attending college: "It has been hypothesized that as more women earn bachelor's degrees, the worth of the degree has declined—thereby causing 'degree creep,' in which advanced degrees are needed as entry level credentials to careers." Conversely, some of those surveyed saw women as identifying college as having more importance for them than men: "Women need a college degree more than men do in order to achieve high earnings."

On the international level, in some countries college is highly populated by women: "The cliché goes that women are more ambitious and more tenacious. However, academic careers are often connected with uncertain employment conditions (at least in Europe), and women may be more willing to agree to them." One pointed to a reason why women may study harder than men: "As far as leading in academic performance, sometimes when you are not initially taken seriously, you are more serious about what you undertake."

Evolving expectations for women in relationship to college are certainly part of the equation. As one woman said,

I think the expectations have changed in terms of college and career. Both men and women are expected to know and plan younger and younger to attend college and aspire to careers that require college, and more steps seem to have to fall into place younger and younger than when I was college going age. Talking to young women they seem more comfortable with imagining a path and taking the steps than when I speak to men the same age.

Nevertheless, traditional role assumptions persist. As one respondent said, "My children were raised by a stay-at-home dad, but when asked who cooks and cleans at home they said, 'Mom'—which was a surprise to both my husband and I. We had seen it as shared. The school always called me when they got in trouble or were sick."

Experienced female administrators note that there have been positive changes in higher education: "I do think some of the views on issues have changed—university policies and practices have had to change." In particular, survey respondents noted important changes having to do with human resources policies and Title IX. Additionally, some commented on the impact of female leadership on changes in the curriculum: "Women have influenced curricula, including the growth of gender and women's studies programs."

Visible female leadership in administration and with the faculty have had a positive impact. "There is at least a perception that more diverse ways of leading have gained traction, and there are female role models, for female students." As one respondent commented, "I do believe that students are more likely to seek help from faculty and administrators who look like them or relate to, which means the demand for co-curricular support has significantly increased. I think it has changed overall role perception in terms of career, family life, relationships, and economic contributions."

In the next chapter, the analysis turns to the global context for the rise of women in higher education.

## DISCUSSION QUESTIONS

1. What were the political and economic pressures that led to an increase of women in post-secondary education?
2. What might be some of the causes behind the disparity in financial aid debt for men and women?
3. In what ways do institutional type and discipline complicate the evaluation of the progress of women faculty members?
4. What are some of the factors that have impacted women and men's attendance in college?
5. In what ways might the tenure and promotion process for faculty disadvantage women?

*Chapter Two*

# Global Perspectives on Women, Education, and Literacy

In this chapter the analysis of women in post-secondary education is broadened to provide an important international perspective. While there are certainly parallels with America in the historical rise of women in academia, especially in England, there is also significant divergence. The ways in which women adapted throughout history to restricted and forbidden access to education and knowledge through individual and group learning, reading, and writing is repeated globally. Statistics on comparative levels of basic skills, gendered STEM disciplines, and female political leadership are all similar to those found in the United States.

The global analysis of education involves central issues for women, including birth rates, contraceptive use, religious beliefs, cultural contexts, and economic development. One key challenge consistent around the globe is the relationship among the factors of childbirth rate, poverty, and education. The successful equalizing of women's participation in post-secondary education worldwide has occurred, but obstacles persist in achieving meaningful access, and equality in employment compensation.

While women who do not attend college are disproportionately disadvantaged economically, at the same time men still on average benefit more from higher education. This is a crucial point: the gender gap favors women in higher education, but men in the overall labor market. Men are less likely than women to earn a college degree, but despite earning more college degrees, women still have worse subsequent employment outcomes.

## BACKGROUND

In his early book on the history of women's education, Bremner (1897) describes the 19th-century period as more of a revival of women's education than the beginning of learning. In Europe from monastic times, before formal education was available, women were involved in various forms of skilled activity working as translators, transcribers, and writers. Much of this activity was done by women in religious orders, and repressed when made public. For instance, with the destruction of nunneries by Henry VIII in England the scholarly work typically done by nuns ceased.

As in the United States, in England access to formal higher education began around the middle of the 19th century. Queen's College opened in 1848, giving women "an improved system of female education," and a year later in 1849 the College of Preceptors also admitted female students. Bedford College in 1849 provided a rare residence hall for women, and was actually financially subsidized by Parliament. Similar to what occurred at elite colleges in America, Newnham College was formed in 1871 to allow women to sit in on Cambridge lectures, but the women were not allowed to be formal members of the university. Girton College started in 1881 and was eventually given permission to allow female students to sit for degree examinations.

Annie Rogers, in her first-person account (1938), traces the origin of women's education at Oxford to the Delegacy of Local Examinations who, citing Cambridge, asked for the power to test women starting in 1870. Rogers herself was on the list three years later in 1873. For 30 years the university apparently took little responsibility for its resident women students. According to Rogers, "As far as the University was concerned, any woman could come to Oxford, behave as badly as she liked, and leave with a certificate which she might claim to be the equivalent of a degree" (p. 24). In 1910 a Delegacy for Women Students was started and not dissolved until women became full members of the university.

As in America, one reason for the eventual permitting of women into the university was that parents increasingly understood that their daughters might need to earn a living, and college would be useful. Oxford awarded degrees to small numbers of women by separate instruction in 1920, and Cambridge as well much later in 1948. In 1963-64 women accounted for 16% of Oxford students, and at Cambridge less than 10% (Malkiel, 2016).

The University of London was the first institution in the United Kingdom to offer equal educational opportunities to women starting in 1878. Professional associations such as the Ladies Educational Society and the National Union for Improving the Education of Women also grew alongside the new educational institutions (Bremner, 1897).

In the larger British Empire, women made inroads into higher education. At the University of Edinburgh in 1864 and St. Andrews in 1865 women were allowed to take examinations without university instruction. In 1868, St. Andrews also started the first educational association for women, the Association for the Promotion of the Higher Education for Women. Legislation in 1892 required the general opening of admissions to female students, which led to both mixed and segregated higher education at existing institutions in Scotland (Bremner, 1897). In Canada, Queen's University admitted women in 1880, McGill University and University of Toronto followed in 1884. At the University of British Columbia, women were enrolled from its inception in 1915.

By the 1960s, the American Civil Rights, Women's, and Antiwar movements were extremely influential in Europe, and cries for women's education forced public policy measures. The Report of the Committee on Higher Education in 1963 made the case for the landmark expansion of British universities, tripling capacity, and promoting higher education access for all. It was estimated at the time that only 5% of the population attended university (Malkiel, 2016).

Oxford and Cambridge were both pressured in this context to change. One key driver of change at Oxford and Cambridge was the recognition that the new coeducational universities in England were popular with the public and in the long run would draw many of the best students away from the historic elite colleges. The Report of the Commission of Inquiry considered implications of expanded access for Oxford, and the Bridges Syndicate followed at Cambridge, discussing specifically the need to increase the number of undergraduate female students. By the 21st century only three women's colleges remained at Cambridge (Malkiel, 2016).

## GLOBAL STATISTICS ON WOMEN AND EDUCATION

### Participation

On the international scene, female participation in higher education overall has increased and currently surpasses that of males in almost all developed countries. Since 1990, the global attendance of women in higher education increased at a faster rate than that of men, enabling enrollment ratios of men and women to reach parity by the turn of the century. Subsequently, the global participation of women has exceeded that of men, shifting gender disparity from a male to female advantage. In 2012, the global tertiary enrollment of women to men was 1.08, reflecting a gender disparity highly favoring women (United Nations Statistics Division, 2015).

In some countries such as Canada and Korea, women are an overwhelming majority in higher education (Figure 2.1).

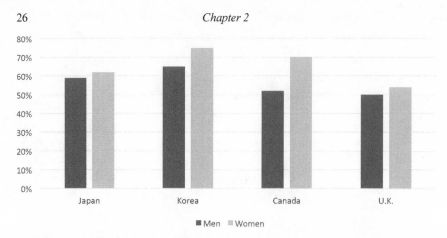

**Figure 2.1.  Tertiary Degree by Gender (24–35 years old).** *OECD, 2018.*

While according to an UNESCO report, the world overall has achieved the target of gender parity at all levels except tertiary education, this is not true of all country and income groups. Only 66% of countries in the world have achieved gender parity in primary education, 45% in lower secondary, and 25% in upper secondary (UNESCO, 2018).

Almost all countries in the Office of Economic Cooperation and Development (OECD) see more women than men in college and a growing gender gap among undergraduates that favors women (OECD, 2018). Of the 17 OECD countries with consistent tertiary schooling enrollment data for the years 1985 and 2002, only four of them (France, Portugal, Sweden, and the United States) had a ratio of male-to-female undergraduates that was below equal in 1985. By 2002, higher education enrollment of women outnumbered that of men in eleven additional countries, including Austria, Belgium, Denmark, Finland, Ireland, Italy, Netherlands, Norway, New Zealand, Spain, and the United Kingdom (Goldin, Katz & Kuziemko, 2006). As Southern Asia moves toward closing the gap, sub-Saharan Africa is the only region where women still do not enroll in or graduate from higher education at the same rates as men (UNESCO, 2018).

## Birthrates

The link between the growing participation of women in education and reduced birth rates is clear. At the beginning of the 19th century, the typical American woman had between seven and eight births in her lifetime. America's pattern of birth began to change greatly by mid-century, which coincided with the very large increase in women's college attendance. Albelda and Tilly (1997) claim that there are three main obstacles for girls in pursuing education: the politics of education, poverty, and pregnancy. For high school girls, the biggest barrier for those who are disadvantaged is pregnancy. This fact is why public policy regarding abortion (*Roe v. Wade*, 1973) has broad social implications beyond the moral/religious debate.

Other Western nations typically began their declines in the late 19th century. Scholars explain the reduction in birthrate as resulting from increased urbanization, perceptions of the value of education, rising female employment, compulsory education, as well as declining infant mortality and better birth control (Haines, 2008).

Internationally, the birth rate has declined significantly in the past half century (Figure 2.2).

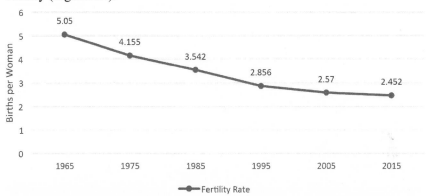

**Figure 2.2. Worldwide Fertility Rate Trend. *UN Population Division, 2017.***

When the proportion of women with secondary schooling doubles, the fertility rate is reduced from 5.3 to 3.9 children (Patrinos, 2008). According to the United Nations, Department of Economic and Social Affairs, Population Division (2017), in almost all regions of the world contraceptives are used by the majority of women who are married, at an average of 63%. Contraceptive use was above 70% in Europe, Latin America, the Caribbean, and Northern America, but below 25% in Middle and Western Africa.

## Employment and Income

While women have surpassed men in higher education globally, they lag significantly behind in employment and income equality. In all OECD and partner countries except Norway and Portugal, employment rates are lower for women than for men, regardless of the educational attainment level. Employment rates are particularly low for women without upper secondary education, reflecting the importance of advanced education for females.

On average across OECD countries, the employment rate of younger women without upper secondary education is 45%, compared to 71% for their male peers. Across all levels of educational attainment, the gender gap in earnings persists. A particularly large gender gap in earnings is strong between male and female full-time workers with higher education—women earn only 74% as much as tertiary-educated men (OECD, 2018). Figure 2.3 displays the relative wages of women compared to men in four specific countries.

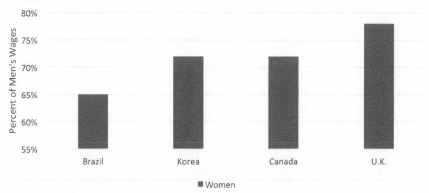

**Figure 2.3.    Women's Wage Comparison to Men (Age 25–64).** *OECD, 2018.*

While women who do not attend college are disproportionately disadvantaged economically, men still benefit more from higher education. On average, the total lifetime advantage for a tertiary-educated man is estimated at $319,600, while the total benefit for a tertiary-educated woman is $234,000 (OECD, 2018).

In this way, the gender gap favors women in education, but men in the labor market. Men are less likely than women to attain a college degree, but despite better educational attainment, women still have worse employment outcomes. On average across OECD countries, 80% of tertiary-educated young women are employed, compared with 89% of young men with the same education, and the disparity increases among those with lower educational attainment. According to OECD, this pay disparity reflects the gender gap observed between high- and low-paying fields of study at the higher education level, but may also result from women's greater likelihood of going through periods of inactivity or unemployment because of family responsibilities, which may delay salary increases (OECD, 2018).

## Science, Technology, Engineering, and Mathematics (STEM)

Although women outnumber men as college graduates in many countries, they lag behind in completing science, technology, engineering and mathematics (STEM) degrees. For example, in Chile, Ghana and Switzerland, women account for less than one-quarter of all STEM degrees. By contrast, in a few countries such as Albania, Algeria and Tunisia, women are more likely than men to earn a STEM degree (UNESCO, 2018). The differences in how men and women select their field of study in graduate programs closely reflect those found at the bachelor's level.

Some scholars (Bank, 2007; May, 2008) focus on the disparity in gender balance in the hard sciences. Women are not under-represented in all STEM fields, but mostly in technical fields such as engineering, manufacturing and construction. Conversely, women are over-represented in the health fields, which many would argue require as much scientific knowledge as other fields, but generally lead to jobs that could be qualified as so-called "care professions," in which women are over-represented (OECD, 2018).

Women are clearly underrepresented in fields related to science and engineering, and overrepresented in education and health fields (Figure 2.4).

One important positive indicator is the diversity of students observed in doctoral programs—the share of women in doctoral programs has increased in the past decade, on average by 2.5% between 2005 and 2016, reaching 48% in 2016. Nevertheless, on average about a third of the women, and half of the men, who pursue doctoral studies entered a STEM field of study. Among these fields, men are twice as likely as women to pursue a doctorate in engineering, manufacturing and construction, and three times as likely to enter a doctoral program in information and communication technologies (OECD, 2018). Women are also underrepresented in STEM research. Women account for 30% of all researchers—an increase compared to previous decades but still far from parity (United Nations Statistics Division, 2015).

Despite enjoying better access to tertiary education than ever before, women continue to face challenges for involvement in some fields of study traditionally dominated by men. This international pattern is consistent with the one found in America, and is particularly so in the case of engineering, and to a lesser extent science, among countries with data for the period 2005–2012. Among male graduates, on average, one in five graduated in

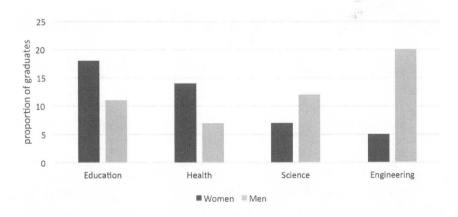

**Figure 2.4.   Women's Representation by Discipline Worldwide.** *UN Statistics Division, 2015.*

engineering compared to one out of 20 women graduates. In 2011, women constituted 30% of all researchers worldwide. This figure has remained almost constant over the past decade, highlighting the lack of progress toward gender parity in this area (United Nations Statistics Division, 2015).

## Gender Skills Comparison

One reason commonly pointed to for gender differences in STEM disciplines has been assumed better male mathematics skills. On the other hand, it has been widely documented that women tend to read more than men (see Chapter 5 for more on this topic). The OECD notes that men and women (25–64 years old) have similar levels of literacy, although men tend to have slightly higher math skills.

Men are also more likely to use information and communications technology skills than women, particularly computer programming. On average across OECD countries, less than 10% of adults over age 15 have recently used a programming language. In all countries, men are at least 50% more likely to have used programming than women (OECD, 2018). Given the importance of computer programming in the technology sector, this indicator is important to watch when considering gains by women in higher education.

Internationally, there is a gender gap in educational achievement in different subjects, and this gap increases as students age. At the primary level, boys and girls do equally well in mathematics and science but girls have a clear advantage in reading. At the secondary level, while girls maintain their advantage in reading, a gap in favor of boys emerges in mathematics (OECD, 2014).

Girls before college appear to be narrowing the gaps in achievement in mathematics where boys have historically held an advantage. Gender differences in science performance showed much narrower gaps than in mathematics and reading for most countries or areas—both OECD and non-OECD— and in most cases the gaps were not statistically significant (OECD, 2014).

Standardized assessments of academic readiness in specific subjects tell a more complex story. Results from one global reading assessment showed that girls outperformed boys in every participating country. The OECD average score for reading performance was 478 points for boys and 515 for girls (a gender gap of 38 score points, which is roughly equivalent to one year of schooling).

Performance in mathematics was also characterized by gender differences, but tended to be smaller and less systematic than those related to reading. Boys performed better in mathematics than girls in the majority of countries that participated in the Program for International Student Assessment (PISA) survey (52 out of 65 countries or areas). The average OECD score in mathematics was 499 for boys and 489 for girls (a 10-point gender gap), while for non-OECD countries or areas, the average score was 453 for boys versus 448 for girls (a five-point gap). In contrast to what was observed for reading, the gender gaps were not significant in many countries. In 13 countries, the gender disparities were actually in the favor of girls, but the size of the gaps was small.

The wide gender disparity in student reading achievement is a striking fact of cross-national learning assessments. But reading comprehension disparities seem to change over time and continue to develop after formal education, reaching a peak at around 30 years old. The ways in which skills develop are influenced by the education and employment paths pursued by men and women. According to one study, the facts about gender differences in skills may be more complicated than the accepted narrative suggests (UNESCO, 2018). Furthermore, recent research concentrates on effective curricula and activities to engage girls with STEM in a positive way that may encourage change (Sullivan, 2019).

## Leadership

Internationally, one measure of change for women is to look at their political participation. Overall, women's share of parliamentary or representative government seats remains low, although it varies across regions from 17.5% and 18% in South Asia and the Arab States, respectively, to 29% in Latin America and Caribbean and OECD countries (UNDP, 2018). Within parliaments, only the Nordic countries come close to equal representation, with women making up 41% of their single-house parliaments. In all other regions, fewer than three in ten parliamentarians are women (Inter-Parliamentary Union, 2017). As of October 2017, out of 193 UN countries, 11 had a woman serving as head of state, and 12 had a woman as head of government (UN Women, 2017).

The political views of women political leaders tend to differ from men. According to UNESCO (2018), women in leadership positions usually favor the equitable redistribution of resources more than men. Legislatures with a higher share of women on average have a tendency to support health, education and social welfare spending over defense spending. Across 103 countries, those that mandated a percentage of women in their legislatures spent 3.4% more on social welfare (Chen, 2010). Nevertheless, the continuing dominance of men in decision-making government posts limits the ability of women to influence policy at all levels (UNESCO, 2018).

The feminization of the teaching workforce in most countries is a well-known phenomenon internationally, but less attention is paid to the continued imbalance of men in educational leadership positions. Women often make up the majority of civil servants generally in particular countries, but have a tendency to be concentrated in positions with less authority. In OECD countries, women represent 57% of the government workforce, but 65% are in secretarial positions, 35% middle manager positions, and only 27% of the top manager positions (OECD and EUPAN, 2015).

In India, 20% of academic deans were women, as were 23% of department heads or directors. In sub-Saharan African countries, women held 13% of dean and 18% of department head or director roles (Singh, 2008). In Europe, 18% of full university professors are women (Vernos, 2013), in India, 26% (Morely and Crossouard, 2014) and in Australia, 27% (Universities Australia, 2017).

As of 2009, only 13% of higher education institutions in 27 European Union countries were headed by women (Morley, 2014). A survey of Commonwealth countries showed that, in 2006, women were the executive heads of 9% of 107 higher education institutions in India, and just 1% of 81 higher education institutions in sub-Saharan African countries.

## International Development, Policy, and Poverty

Tembon and Fort (2008) point out that in the international context, gender equality is not just a women's issue, but an economic development issue that has an impact extending beyond the education sector into the areas of law, health, agriculture and infrastructure. The economic benefit that comes from educating women for one additional year of schooling is estimated to be 11% in developing countries, compared to 7% in industrial countries. Providing girls with an extra year of schooling increases their subsequent wages by 10 to 20% (Patrinos, 2008).

In terms of policy, the international community has been formally committed to achieving gender equality since the establishment of the United Nations. Chapter I of the UN Charter lists as one of its purposes the effort to achieve international cooperation through "promoting and encouraging respect for human rights and for fundamental freedoms for all without distinction as to race, sex, language or religion" (United Nations, 1945).

More recently, the 2030 Agenda for Sustainable Development commits countries to gender equality throughout all 17 of the Sustainable Development Goals (SDGs). Furthermore, the Education 2030 Framework for Action, the international community's roadmap toward achieving goals, recognizes that gender equality is essential if the right to education is to be extended to all. Nevertheless, the 2030 Agenda is not legally binding (UNESCO, 2018).

Generally, there is a wide variation of emphasis and achievement in the education sectors of the Asian and Pacific regions (UNESCO, 1992). As a result, UNESCO has focused organizationally on gathering global information on gender inequality with attention on accountability.

Achieving gender equality in education involves complex processes and the efforts of many actors. Accountability can help ensure all are functioning as they should. Accountability is a process that helps individuals or institutions meet responsibilities and reach goals. For the purposes of this review, it can be understood as having three main elements: firstly, the actor must have clearly defined responsibilities; secondly, the actor must have an obligation to provide an account of how responsibilities have been met; and thirdly, there must be a legal, political, social or moral justification for the obligation to account. (UNESCO, 2018, p. 37)

Three global treaties are particularly relevant to gender equality in education. First, the 1979 Convention on the Elimination of All Forms of Discrimination against Women (CEDAW) is a treaty with regard to the legal obligations of governments toward gender equality in education. Articles 2 and 3 set forth measures that states should take to eliminate discrimination. Article 5 requires nations to eliminate all gender stereotyping, prejudices, and discriminatory practices. Article 10 lays out state obligations and establishes acceptable norms, including in regard to equality in access and quality of education, and access to information on family planning. Article 16 prohibits child marriage. Although 189 states have ratified CEDAW, many countries have noted reservations which undermine commitment to the treaty.

The Convention against Discrimination in Education (CADE) is the only treaty specific to the field of education, and comprehensively covers discrimination. CADE prohibits discrimination by gender both in access and quality of education. Article 2 permits gender-segregated educational institutions provided that they have the same quality, provide equivalent content, and meet the same standards (Right to Education Initiative, 2018).

Finally, Articles 13 and 14 of the International Covenant on Economic, Social and Cultural Rights (ICESCR) are the foundation of the legal right to education. In elaborating on the guarantee of education for all in Article 13, the treaty states specific practices necessary to provide remedy for discrimination (Right to Education Initiative, 2018).

It is notable that the United States is frequently absent from international treaties, and the only country that has not ratified the Convention on the Rights of the Child. It has not signed CEDAW, CADE, and ICESCR. Furthermore, it has not guaranteed the right to education in its constitution, which means that citizens in the United States lack an important recourse in cases of violation (UNESCO, 2018).

## Poverty

Diane Pearce (1978) is said to have coined the phrase "the feminization of poverty," referring to the fact that women account for an increasingly large proportion of the economically disadvantaged. Poverty is a central women's issue globally. In general, countries with higher rates of illiteracy and lower female participation in formal education are associated with a higher incidence of poverty (UNESCO, 1992).

Gender disparities in poverty are rooted in inequalities in access to economic resources because of typical economic dependency on males. In developing countries laws continue to restrict women's access to land and other financial assets, and often hold cultural traditions limiting control over the household economics. In nearly a third of developing countries, laws fail to guarantee inheritance rights for women. According to one report, even with increased participation in the workforce, for those women who work outside the home, only one in ten married women are consulted on how their own earnings are spent (United Nations Statistics Division, 2015).

Scholars have noted that occupational segregation and women's responsibilities for childcare are key factors in the feminization of poverty. Women are often segregated into lower wage jobs such as teaching, child care, nursing, cleaning and waitressing (Albelda & Tilly, 1997). Furthermore, Kingfisher (2002) argues that the welfare state and neo-liberal reform movements internationally actually tend to reproduce gender roles that hurt women because such public policy depends on women's cheap labor and unpaid domestic work.

Internationally, women's earnings are approximately 70–80% of that of men, and this disparity has much to do with females primarily responsible for child care and domestic chores. In North America, the increase in single mothers has also contributed to the poverty figures—half of all single mothers in the United States have incomes below the poverty line.

An important aspect of the poverty figures is the degree to which children live in poverty. In America for instance, only 27% of the population is under 18, yet children comprise 40% of all poor people. Women make up 62% of the adults in poverty (Kingfisher, 2002). Women are poorer than men in all racial and ethnic groups, but Black and Latina women face particularly high rates of poverty. They are twice as likely as white women to be living in poverty (Albelda & Tilly, 1997).

Some experts argue that poor women have fewer options and models to encourage a life different than the one they were born into (Albelda & Tilly, 1997). Carol Gilligan (1993) notes in her seminal work on human development that women often develop an identity based on a male perspective. As a result, nurturing and caretaking role expectations leave them with less focus on self and advancement. While men are taught autonomy, women are more relational and seek approval. Consequently, for those women living in poverty self-confidence is a central need.

## Education and Social Mobility

Looking at the broader context of social mobility within which the rise of women in college occurred, the question of education's impact on mobility is complex and may be as much associative as causative. In *Low-income Students and the Perpetuation of Inequality: Higher Education in America* (Berg, 2010), the author questioned the impact of education on the mobility of those in a historically lower-class status. In Europe generally data do not show progress in class mobility through education. Especially in the United Kingdom, where there was a very large shift toward public post-secondary education, the social mobility results were disappointing.

Public policy internationally has displayed a consciousness of class, while American higher education has relied on a notoriously less centralized intentional non-system. Only with affirmative action and Title IX policies implemented at the end of the twentieth century did American higher education become directly purposeful in addressing inequality in educational opportunity.

The issue of social mobility is probably an even greater matter of attention on the international scene than in America. In *Persistent Inequality: Changing Educational Attainment in Thirteen Countries*, the authors asked the question of to what extent socio-economic characteristics and education changed over time and found that expansion has not generally entailed greater equality of educational opportunity (Shavit & Blossfeld, 1993). Internationally, there still exists a clear connection between social class and educational attainment.

Some scholars have looked at the overall international economic impact of education in relationship to class and claim that the sorting function of education is important for businesses needing quick ways to place new employees (Wolfe, 2002). Contrary to popular belief, increased public education does not always lead to better national economies. Those countries which have concentrated most on elevating the education levels of their population have grown more slowly than those which have devoted less attention to education because skilled workers are less important to economic growth than other factors making up the total economy.

Generally, the increased investment in higher education has led to higher participation among the upper and middle classes. The impact of broader higher education is particularly evident in England where the upper classes increasingly participated in higher education: from 33% in 1960 to 79% in 1994. At the same time, those from lower-class family backgrounds increased involvement from only 4 to 12%.

In America in 1972, those from the top 25% family income and lowest 25% in school achievement entered college at the rate of 57.9%, while in the same year the highest-achieving lower 25% economic class went to college at the rate of 69.7%. In 1992, the rate of low-achieving high-income students rose to 77.3%. Thus by 1992, those from upper-class families who performed poorly in secondary school entered college at the same rate as those from poor families who performed well in secondary school (Wolfe, 2002).

Regardless, the context of women and education of various classes in America and other developed countries is far different than in the rest of the world. As Illich (1983) points out, "Whatever his or her claims of solidarity with the Third World, each American college graduate has had an education costing an amount five times greater than the median life income of half of humanity."

## CONCLUSION

Education for women is a form of emancipation. This is the conclusion that Martin and Goodman (2004) made after following teacher leaders in the United Kingdom investigating how they make sense of their lives, educational philosophies, and the inevitable tensions arising when women become change agents. In reviewing the dense and wide-ranging statistics on women in higher education globally, one is struck with how advancements are tied closely to political, cultural, and economic factors.

Women globally have become the largest group of new politically empowered people. Their participation in education has changed every discipline in higher education. The increase in women's academic scholarship alone has had a revolutionary impact regardless of the author's politics. Internationally, women's legal rights and protections have increased, particularly in terms of greater control over reproductive rights. Women's access to voting since 1900 has approximately doubled, and their participation has brought different approaches and focus to political action (Bucur, 2018).

Nevertheless, there is general recognition of challenges and uneven progress in globally educating women. Although in the last third of the 20th century women internationally made great strides in higher education, globally the introduction of equality in education through legislation and national policy has been problematic (Erskine & Wilson, 1999). Outside the world's rich countries, men still have the greater educational opportunities. While great strides have been made internationally regarding the education of women, severe problems still persist.

There are still many very troubling indicators of broad gender inequity. In specific countries such as India, historically only Brahmins had privilege and access to education (Dupta, 2000). According to some estimates, approximately 25 million girls worldwide, and one million girls in India alone, are killed before birth as a result of sex selective abortions (Population Research Institute, 2018). A sad indication of the fate of many females is a government survey conducted by the Indian government in 2007 which found that 48.4% of young women said they did not want to be female (Sabni, 2017).

It is important to note that it is not just girls and women attending school that is key, but that the education be of high quality. In fact, improved quality in education pays even bigger dividends in developing countries and has a significant impact on economic growth. Simply building schools in developing countries does not necessarily impact human capital growth; in fact, low-quality schools many actually decrease growth (Hanushek, 2008).

A UNESCO report lists six indicators of gender inequality by specific domains: educational opportunities, gender norms, institutions outside education, legislation and policies, resource distribution, and teaching and learning practices. This approach recognizes the complex nature of educational disadvantage, and the need for a broad cultural and political approach to encourage change for the better (UNESCO, 2018).

One example of this complexity is the educational impact of public health and menstrual hygiene on the education of women. The lack of adequate sanitary care for adolescent girls leads to missed days at school. In Bangladesh, 41% of schoolgirls aged 11 to 17 reported missing 2.8 days of school per menstrual cycle (Alam et al., 2017). The global visibility of the issue has increased in recent years (Sommer and Sahin, 2013), but financing policy measures on sanitation were targeted at women in only 11 of 74 countries surveyed (WHO and UN Water, 2017).

A study in rural areas of Ethiopia, Kenya, Mozambique, Rwanda, Uganda and Zambia found that less than 20% of schools had recommended menstrual hygiene services (Morgan et al., 2017). Data on water, sanitation, and hygiene expenditures in rural Kenyan primary schools showed that expenditures averaged only $1.83 per student per year (Alexander et al., 2016). Analysis from four territories in India between 2007 and 2015 found that providing separate female toilets in schools was positively associated with school enrollment (Ray & Datta, 2017).

Violence against women affects all societies, and in some regions childhood marriage and high adolescence birth rates undermine the opportunities for many young women and girls. In South Asia, 29% of women between the ages of 20 and 24 were married before their 18th birthday. High adolescent birth rates, early motherhood, and poor and unequal access to pre- and post-natal health services result in a high maternal mortality ratio (UNDP, 2018).

In regard to the gendered disciplines reported in this chapter, faculty and administrators interviewed for this book commented that "historically, women have not been in STEM fields with certain notable exceptions largely due to societal norms and ways young girls are introduced to different types of work usually in the 'caring' professions like teaching and nursing." One respondent noted one possible reason for the continued difference: "In psychology, there's an extensive literature contending that stereotype threats and beliefs about inferior ability discourage women from majoring in STEM."

Faculty and administrators pointed to the messaging regarding women and STEM that begins in childhood: "I think despite dramatic changes in the number of women in education some societal things persist. I was told by a high school teacher that girls could not do physics in the 1980s despite the fact it was my 4th science I had taken in high school. I excelled at science and social science. I chose history and stayed with history despite it being dominated by men." Internationally, as seen earlier in this chapter, the same sort of gendered disciplinary pattern persists. "In Europe there are surveys that indicated that the reasons are linked with how kids grow up, what they play, what their parents encourage them to be interested in—dolls vs. cars."

The next chapter looks more deeply into the history of women's higher education, especially in relationship to the development of different types of institutions, including women-only, coeducational, and coordinate institutions. The social forces that shaped the development of these colleges will be considered. Finally, four specific American institutions will be examined which represent Catholic women's colleges, elite women-only colleges, and an urban social research institution.

## DISCUSSION QUESTIONS

1. In what ways is educating women improving society as a whole worldwide?
2. Which are the key organizations and documents in promoting women's education worldwide?
3. What are the linkages between poverty, birthrates, and women's education?
4. What are the trends in regard to STEM fields for women internationally?
5. Describe the issues surrounding the gender skills debate.

## Chapter Three

# Women's and Coeducational Colleges

In this chapter, women's and coeducational colleges are studied closely because they play a central role in understanding the historical surge of female students in American colleges. Highlighted are their specific institutional strengths and weaknesses in meeting the needs of the growing student body of women new to higher education. Additionally, individual institutions of particular note are considered to illustrate the expansion of women's education in the extremely varied and diverse American landscape of post-secondary education. In regard to women-only colleges, a primary question for the reader to keep in mind is what ways specific approaches used in these institutions might be adopted by coeducational universities today to better serve the evolving student body.

The development and growth of women's and coeducational institutions in America is represented in Figure 3.1.

The dominance of men-only institutions in the early 19th century was quickly surpassed by coeducational institutions, many of them land grant colleges funded by the Morrill Act of 1862. Throughout the 20th century, there was a slow fade in the number of gender-exclusive colleges, with the fate of women's colleges paralleling men's closely up to the present day.

In the 1960s there were more than 200 women's colleges in the United States, and at the present time there are fewer than 50. While the great expansion in involvement of women in postsecondary education was accomplished largely through coeducational institutions, women's colleges played an influential role in the development of curricula, student activities, and student services specifically aimed at female students.

**Figure 3.1.   Number and Type of Higher Education Institutions Trend.** *Tidball, Smith, Tidball, & Wold-Wendall, 1999.*

## WOMEN'S COLLEGES

The history of women's colleges in America can be traced to the founding of Salem College in 1772, first as a primary school, and later as the influential Mount Holyoke established in 1837. Women-only colleges arose out of multiple emerging social forces of the time period, most importantly the lack of access to male institutions. Exclusion allowed women's colleges to consider the specific needs of female learners. Horowitz (1984) argues that the "Seven Sister" women's colleges (Mount Holyoke, Vassar, Wellesley, Smith, Radcliffe, Bryn Mawr, and Barnard) all started with the advantage of missions focused on educating women.

Women's colleges were at first typically Protestant; only in the late 19th century did the colleges allow a trickle of Jewish and Catholic students to be admitted. They began by attracting middle-class women who sought to become teachers, but by the 1890s those from wealthy families who had no immediate need of a post-college career also began to attend. This entrance of a new type of student into women's colleges subsequently changed the curriculum and student life, causing some division between the new more affluent population and the hard studying, less privileged students known often derisively as "grinds" (Horowitz, 1984).

Indeed, over the late 19th century and into the 20th century, women's colleges debated the question of which population of young women they should be serving (Mount Holyoke College, 1937). For instance, one issue of the Mount Holyoke alumnae magazine included a discussion about the composition of the student body, offering an academic versus finishing school perspective: "Why should we aim for 'finish' and cushioned comfort, offerings all too common and meaningless, when we have realities of mind and

**Figure 3.2. Seniors marching to chapel, Mt. [Mount] Holyoke College, South Hadley, Mass., (1908).** *Detroit Publishing Company photograph collection (Library of Congress).*

spirit to offer?" (Mount Holyoke College, 1933, p. 216). From 1900 to 1920 the change in the student body with more affluent female students attracted to the "college life" and socializing led to conflict with serious academic faculty (Palmieri, 1995).

Many of the women's colleges had a clear social advocacy goal that steered clear of an emphasis on refining women from wealthy families. "This means that no young woman should be graduated from college without an underlying conviction that both her work, if she is gainfully employed, and her leisure time and volunteer activities, have social and civic, as well as personal aspects and obligations" (Adams, 1923, p.15).

The Settlement House movement in America had an influence on the purpose and curriculum of early women's colleges. First founded by Jane Addams, Hull House in Chicago in 1889 was a dwelling in a poor urban neighborhood staffed by educated women offering community programs such as childcare and medical services geared toward women. The stated purpose was to share the benefits of the education of more affluent women with immigrant women. In turn the women volunteers benefited by gaining an understanding of the plight of poor and immigrant women (Turpin, 2016).

As a result of this social advocacy, Smith College graduates created the New York Settlement House, which was modeled on British examples, and practiced the social education of college women through work in communities. Wellesley, Smith, and Vassar successfully sent the most women into settlement work. Social work was a field open to women because it was vocational and also a civic duty. College clubs and organizations such as the Young Women's Christian Association (YWCA), the Charity Organization Society, and the College Settlements Association (CSA) were popular in women's colleges (Faragher, 1988).

Of all the secular women's colleges founded in the late 19th century, only Wellesley from the beginning committed to having a predominately female faculty and president. Unlike many of the other colleges, women scholars at Wellesley were regarded as genuine intellectuals, challenging the traditional domestic roles of the time, and creating a cohesive women's culture of intellectualism, feminism, and social reform. Female faculty believed that a time of transition in American culture required a new set of ideals for middle-class women, or what was termed "symmetrical womanhood."

Developing healthy women outside of the parameters of marriage was a goal, along with setting the stage for possible community activism and a career. Furthermore, the Wellesley faculty challenged expectations about middle-class women, especially about physical beauty. Instead the focus was on women's usefulness to society (Palmieri, 1995).

The Seven Sister Colleges spurred the development of a number of others throughout America, especially in the East and South, where two-thirds of the early women's colleges were located. As opposed to men-only institutions, women's colleges were initially much more restrictive on students, with constant supervision by the faculty, strict rules structuring their days, regular religious devotion, and often a physically secluded campus location. According to some observers, while men typically had great freedom in college leading often to social excess, in many ways women's colleges were said to be similar to nunneries (Horowitz, 1984).

Additionally, women's colleges often directly opposed a concentration on a domestic science curriculum. Bryn Mawr College leadership was against general vocational training for women, and instead emphasized the arts and sciences (Turpin, 2016). A key challenge throughout this developmental period of women's education was to relate the purposes of liberal academic study to 19th century American women's conventional domestic and limited work roles (Solomon, 1985).

Although the Seven Sister institutions provided models for others, quality became a problem at many of the spinoff colleges they inspired. One estimate in 1875 was that out of 209 schools, only a half-dozen met male college levels of quality (Woody, 1929). In 1852 the American Women's Education Association was formed with the purpose of setting standards for the women's college movement. The growing number of women's colleges eventually raised the bar on educational excellence and institutional reputations throughout the latter half of the century (Rudolph, 1990).

Mount Holyoke became a prototype for many women's institutions. Mary Lyon, who led Mount Holyoke, instituted two key organizational strategies: very low teacher salaries, and a cooperative labor system in which students did cooking and domestic chores. She also avoided fundraising from wealthy donors, which was a common practice at other colleges (Turpin, 2016). Expressing the philosophy of Mount Holyoke College, Mary Emma Woolley, the president, said in 1919, "The higher education of women is a feministic movement, the natural expression of a fundamental principle that is that women being first of all human beings, even before they are feminine have a share in the inalienable right of human beings to self-development" (Marks, 1955, p. 80).

It was seen by some during the second half of the 19th century as a danger to have women separated from families and close parental oversight. College life at women's colleges often led to independence and intense female friendships, and the students graduating confidently expressed opinions that opposed typical views of marriage. Women's colleges had the advantage of developing outside of coeducational colleges where male culture often dominated the overall climate. However, some critics point out that women's colleges were built partly by a limiting negative—they knew they didn't want to be men's colleges (Horowitz, 1984).

One challenge women-only colleges encountered early on was that female faculty members lacked the same position and autonomy enjoyed by their male colleagues. Male professors often had single-family homes supplied by the college, while women faculty only had rooms in student housing with the added responsibility of monitoring the students. The requirement to look after students took time away from their own scholarship. Female faculty were also paid far less, and the unequal compensation was such that women faculty had trouble affording, if even allowed, to live on their own away from the campus. Furthermore, women faculty were generally not respected academically and were often called "teacher," while only men were addressed as "professor."

By the 1880s women faculty members began to gain greater respect in society, yet the structural inequality persisted in colleges. This changed by 1910, and women began living off campus, often in pairs, creating an outside intellectual culture as this arrangement became more common. The transformation of living off campus led to the professionalization of women faculty (Horowitz, 1984).

## COORDINATE COLLEGES

At elite institutions, "coordinate" or linked women's colleges were a typical model used to accommodate women in college without disrupting the male-only institutions. At Harvard, access by women was slow and met a great deal of resistance. Harvard President Charles W. Eliot in an 1869 address declared that he had no intention of admitting women because the world knew "next to nothing about the natural mental capacities of the female sex" and that it would take "generations of civil freedom and social equality to obtain the data necessary for an adequate discussion of women's natural tendencies, tastes and capabilities" (Malkiel, 2016).

Radcliffe College began in 1878 as the "Annex," or formally "The Society, for the Collegiate Instruction of Women." Initially after a four-year course, a certificate was earned by female students who attended the Annex. Only "instruction," nothing more, was promised to female students. Later in 1893 with an endowment and legal link to Harvard it became Radcliffe College.

At first only men from Harvard were faculty, and there was no separate physical building for women students. In this way, President Eliot and other leaders at Harvard publicly resisted women's formal education. Radcliffe, as the Annex, lacked any distinct components to its education; it simply met local demand for the high-level education of women (Turpin, 2016).

It wasn't until 1894 that Radcliffe College was chartered as a women's college with visiting Harvard faculty serving as "visitors," and Harvard's president countersigning the Radcliffe diplomas. Two months after Radcliffe was commissioned, the Harvard Board of Overseers voted that they would, under no circumstances, give bachelor's degrees to women. Radcliffe was to be a non-coeducational women's version of Harvard. Administration termed what eventually became mixed classrooms as "joint instruction," but this was not formalized until 1947 for upper-class students, and then for first year students in 1950 (Malkiel, 2016).

From the start, although Radcliffe benefited from Harvard faculty instruction, it was comparatively lacking in student housing, financial aid, athletics, and student activities. It wasn't until 1999 that Harvard and Radcliffe finally legally combined, becoming one institution. The merger discussion was difficult with many from the Radcliffe side skeptical about Harvard's willingness to accommodate female students.

Specifically, during the debate at the end of the 20th century when merger was actively discussed, skeptics pointed to the long history of male-only faculty members. In fact, there had been only one tenured female faculty member at Harvard since 1948, and a handful of lecturers. Additionally, many wondered if the conservative male faculty members accustomed to teaching only men would give sufficient academic respect to female students.

With the formal union, Radcliffe College effectively went out of business, although a new Radcliffe Institute for Advanced Study with a commitment to the study of women and society was formed as part of Harvard (Malkiel, 2016)

At Columbia, Barnard College was created similarly as a female annex in 1889 with Columbia faculty serving as visitors to enforce structural separation from the male institution (Solomon, 1985). As with other women's colleges, the influence of powerful women backers from elite families was key in the formation of Barnard College. In an effort not to offend the sensibilities of male authorities, the rise of the coordinate women colleges with support of prominent citizens was discrete. At first intentionally avoiding out of classroom connections to students, by 1910 both Radcliffe and Barnard built campuses and began to see college life as the essence of the experience for their female students. Evelyn was Princeton's similar attempt at a separate coordinate women's college, but it was unsuccessful and folded in 1897 (Turpin, 2016).

As with male-only institutions, women's colleges often had a religious core mission. According to Turpin (2016), it is often overlooked that female student arrival at college was crucial to creating a new moral and religious ideal for both women and men. In forming women's colleges with a religious center, the primary question asked was, "In relation to God, what does it mean to be female?" Early leaders of women's colleges found that they needed to look anew at moral and practical purposes, given American cultural realities, and often shifted from Protestant evangelicalism to modernism in religious emphasis.

This change in religious affiliation and purpose at colleges marked a swing from a primary relationship to God, to a focus on the human community. For instance, Wellesley sought to produce women equipped and motivated to help construct a godly social order, in part through the profession of social work. At Oberlin, the curriculum espoused the radical belief that female teachers were spiritual equals to male ministers. At both Holyoke and Oberlin, alumnae often went into the society as reformers, or doing religious work which pushed limits, but in a way not too offensive to the traditional order (Turpin, 2016).

Turpin (2016) argues that despite inherited 19th-century assumptions about women and religion being linked, religion at the separate and sometimes linked women's colleges was smaller in influence than at their male counterpart institutions. The emphasis on the moral purpose of education came at the same time that women were also entering public universities. The difference was that in public institutions female students tended to take more responsibly for themselves, and there was less organized protection and coddling of women.

## CATHOLIC WOMEN'S COLLEGES

Roman Catholic colleges are one of the prominent subgroups of women's colleges in America. Historically, access for women in male Catholic colleges was an issue where separatism was informally and formally imposed upon women. The first women's religious order in America to launch a number of Catholic women's colleges was the Sisters of Notre Dame who in 1896 opened the College of Notre Dame, followed in 1900 with Trinity College (Hesse-Biber & Leckenby, 2003).

From the beginning, Catholic women's colleges fixed on asserting the worth of women socially and religiously. In the 1920s American nun educators were prepared in universities outside of the United States such as Oxford, Munich, and the Sorbonne, as well as the best domestic institutions. By 1955 there were 116 Catholic baccalaureate colleges for women, and 24 two-year colleges (Tidball, 1989).

Catholic colleges often focused on traditionally underserved ethnic and lower-class women students and as a result have pioneered innovative deliv-

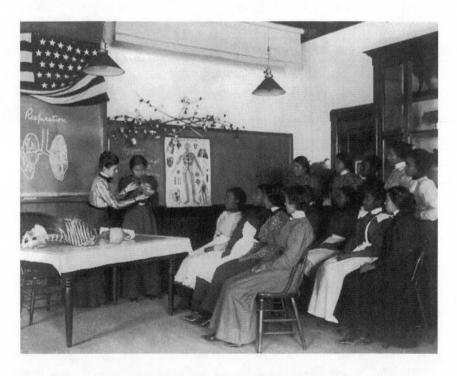

**Figure 3.3.   American Indian and African American students at Hampton Institute, Hampton, Va. (1900?)—women studying human respiratory system.** *Johnston, Frances Benjamin, photographer (Library of Congress).*

ery forms such as weekend college, summers-only colleges, and competency-based credit options. Additionally, Catholic women's colleges often have a high proportion of women presidents and faculty members.

Catholic women's colleges were all heavily influenced in curriculum by the Seven Sister Colleges and their emphasis on educating women and improving society. Changes in these colleges in the 1960s, partially prompted by Vatican Council II, directed students even more toward social action in the world. Overall, some argue that the role of women and feminists in the Catholic church is problematic, and that at times social justice is discussed on these campuses, but not practiced (Hesse-Biber & Leckenby, 2003).

## COEDUCATIONAL COLLEGES

While only the University of Iowa permitted coeducation before the Civil War, the emergence of land-grant universities in the late 19th century, spurred by funding from the Morrill Act of 1862, gave rise to coeducation on a broad level. The first eight state universities to accept women were Iowa (1855), Wisconsin (1867), Kansas, Indiana, Minnesota (1869), Missouri, Michigan and California (1870); of these, Iowa, Kansas, Minnesota, and California admitted women only from their home states (Solomon, 1985). By 1880 over 30% of American colleges admitted women, and by the year 1900, 71% were coeducational (Rudolph, 1990).

When the Morrill Act was implemented, more women were expected to participate in higher education, and as we saw in the first chapter, they did. Scholars argue that the end of slavery led to a general reconsideration of human rights, including those of women to seek education. They also claim that a shift in the purpose of higher education occurred from a sole concentration on personal improvement to one aimed at the larger sense of social responsibility and civic engagement, thus giving colleges a stronger rationale for public funding (Newcomer,1959; Solomon, 1985).

However, many social challenges existed for these newly formed coeducational institutions. For instance, culturally women were expected to be silent in public, and this expectation carried over into college with women prohibited from speaking in front of men in many coeducational classrooms (Rudolph, 1990). It wasn't until 1858 that women at Oberlin were permitted to speak at commencement ceremonies (Solomon, 1985). Western American colleges were generally more open to coeducational opportunities because of a culture in which women worked actively on the family ranch or farm. In 1872 there were ninety-seven major coeducational colleges in America and sixty-seven were in the West.

After the second world war, women's colleges confronted the challenges of changed sexual mores, and new attitudes toward college. Faced with declining applicants, the women's colleges established cooperative arrangements with men's institutions, and Vassar, Sarah Lawrence, and Bennington became coeducational. Post-war women also brought new demands to the colleges with students who were ambitious personally, and out front about their sexuality. In retrospect, Horowitz noted that "women's colleges can be seen as vivid emblems of how Americans once perceived college women, and how women students, alumnae, and faculty came to perceive themselves" (Horowitz, 1984, p. 354). After the 1960s women's colleges declined in number, and virtually all women's and men's institutions convened committees to study the "coeducational question."

Elite private men's institutions were very slow to move to coeducation, and as we saw earlier, staved off having women in their colleges by creating separate, linked institutions. Given the social movements of the 1960s it would have been very difficult for elite colleges to resist change forever. Nevertheless, the leadership at the time, to varying degrees by institution, had to lead the way in institutional change. With sometimes great resistance and complication between 1969 and 1974, coeducation came into being at these intuitions.

In the 1960s Princeton was the first Ivy League college to consider coeducation with the release of the highly influential Patterson Report in 1968. With great thoroughness the report argued for coeducation, stating simply, "Princeton would be a better university if women were admitted to the undergraduate college." The comprehensive report directly influenced Yale, as well as Oxford and Cambridge in the United Kingdom. The Princeton report most importantly detailed a far lower financial cost for the transition to coeducation than had been anticipated because of existing capacity on the physical campus, in the undergraduate ranks, and already expanding graduate programs. The report also anticipated benefits in the growth of some of the smaller majors in the humanities, and overall better use of faculty resources (Malkiel, 2016).

Furthermore, President Goheen at Princeton argued that if the college failed to coeducate it would become a second-rate institution. The college did face formidable challenges in admitting women to its faculty, and by alumni and students wanting to protect their storied private eating clubs. In 1969 there were only three female professors at Princeton. Suzanne Keller, the first female professor, described receiving an appointment letter addressed to "Dear Sir," as an indication of the cultural shift that was needed at that time. By 1979–80 Princeton increased the number of female tenured faculty to ten (Malkiel, 2016).

Princeton eating clubs were a particular challenge because they were privately owned, including their buildings, and run by dues-paying students and alumni boards. Their deep link to the college's history made the transition to female membership very difficult. While at first not allowed into eating clubs, women students nevertheless outperformed men academically in elections to Phi Beta Kappa, and honors and scholarships (Malkiel, 2016).

Yale University had been educating women graduate students in the arts and sciences and professional schools since 1869—almost a century before their admission was considered at the undergraduate level. In 1892 women were allowed to enter doctoral programs, with the first degrees granted in 1894. In fact, by 1900 Yale graduated more women from doctoral programs than any other American university (Malkiel, 2016).

The reason Yale moved toward admitting women students at the under-graduate level, as with other elite institutions, was the sense that by the 1960s single-sex admission was becoming a competitive liability. Indeed, when Princeton and Yale admitted women, Dartmouth became the only Ivy League school without a coordinate women's college or plans to coeducate, which led to its decline in enrollment. Additionally, an impression that Yale's campus atmosphere resembled a wealthy boy's club called out for modernization. A merger with Vassar ultimately would bring needed curricular changes to the college (Malkiel, 2016).

Like Yale, Vassar was an old institution which opened in 1865 as primarily a preparatory school. Over the years it closed the preparatory division, and became academically well respected in its own right (Malkiel, 2016). Vassar for its part was attracted to merging with Yale because of changing application patterns which confirmed that incoming students from their traditional student base wanted coeducation. Furthermore, increasing numbers of applicants came from coeducational preparatory schools which fed into Vassar, and on top of that, the college had to compete with former elite male-only institutions which now accepted women.

Resistance to the union of Yale and Vassar was strong from alumna at Vassar. For instance, one graduate wrote in a *Life Magazine* article, "How can they contemplate trading an intimate personal environment for the mounting de-personalization of the multiversity?" (Seiberling, 1967). The press covered the arrival of female students in the fall of 1969 on the Yale campus with interest. Female graduate students who had long been at Yale appeared diminished in the uproar over new undergraduate students.

As with many previously men-only institutions, there was a difficult transition period. Some of Yale's private eating and drinking clubs resisted women members, as did the secret societies. The prominent Skull and Bones and Wolf's Head clubs held out in restricting women until 1992. Nevertheless, the first undergraduate women at Yale held their own, academically outscoring men on incoming SAT verbal tests, although lagging behind in the math section. Women also began to rise to leadership positions in student activities and groups (Malkiel, 2016).

Princeton was slower than the other institutions to balance gender in enrollment, possibly because of its conservative reputation and eating clubs as well as a large engineering major. Initially setting a target of 25%, it did not reach 40% female enrollment until 1990, and then 50/50 by 2010.

In terms of men to women student ratios, Princeton in 1969–70 was 19 to 1, and 8 to 1 a year later. Yale was seven to one in 1969–70, five to one the following year. Harvard competitively responded by setting a target of two and a half to one.

Overall, the actions of the big three to move to coeducation influenced other elite privates such as the University of Virginia, Johns Hopkins, Caltech, Brown, Rutgers, and Amherst. Women's colleges watching Vassar and following their lead included Bennington, Sarah Lawrence, and Skidmore. Military academies such as West Point and the Naval Academy began to admit women. By 2015 only four men-only colleges remained. With coeducation also came the pressure to modernize the curriculum, and Women's Studies entered as a discipline (see Chapter 6). Yale started such a program in 1979, and Harvard followed later in 1986 (Malkiel, 2016).

Some women's colleges in the East were fearful that a growth of undergraduate female students at Harvard, Yale, and Princeton might lead to a brain drain at their own institutions. Nevertheless, coeducation was considered by Smith and Wellesley, but these institutions finally decided against it. Some at Smith argued that the coeducation debate was different for women's colleges who would lose first-rate education apart from male competition. Smith abandoned the effort to become coeducational with a 2–1 majority vote. Alumna Gloria Steinem, sensing the point of progress in the higher education of women, wrote in "The Politics of Women" that "our heads are not together enough yet as women to be integrated" (Malkiel, 2016).

Malkiel (2016) in her comprehensive book addresses the questions of why traditional and elite institutions decided to move to coeducation in the late 1960s and early 1970s, and how the change was accomplished. She argues that coeducation resulted not from efforts by women at the time, but by strategic decisions by powerful men. The direction was chosen not based on possible benefits to women, but instead as responses to social pressures, and financial expedience.

Coeducation can be viewed in hindsight as a success in bringing resources to women's education and increasing overall numbers of female students in college. Yet problems persist: coeducation has not corrected biased attitudes on previously male campuses, fields of study are still gendered, and faculty at elite institutions remains unbalanced. At Princeton in 2014–15 for instance, women comprised only 24.6% of the tenured faculty. Regardless, coeducation has become the norm in American higher education with now less than 5% of high school students indicating interest in women's colleges (Malkiel, 2016).

## ARGUMENTS FOR AND AGAINST WOMEN'S COLLEGES

According to Renn (2014), women's colleges overall are in some ways a paradox of supporting gender equity, while at the same time continuing the status quo. While the public's view of women-only colleges has evolved over time, once coeducation became an option, the core issues debated about the value of such institutions are unchanged. There are two general arguments against women's colleges: first, that students don't have the opportunity to learn how to navigate a male world; second, that women's colleges don't provide the best route to equality by missing access to networks of power and influence needed after college.

Advocates of women's colleges point to benefits seen in outcomes: proportionally more scientists and medical doctors as graduates, heightened awareness of women's political issues, and the development of leadership qualities (Renn, 2014). Some studies have indicated women students complaining about a "chilly" campus climate for women on coeducational campuses, which make female-only colleges attractive. Women's colleges often sponsor Women's Studies programs and research centers, which in some ways become an academic arm of the feminist movement. The ratio of female professors and leaders tends to be higher at women's colleges.

Tidball, Smith, Tidball, and Wolf-Wendel (1999) summarize the benefits and characteristics of exemplary women's colleges as providing high expectations, support, a critical mass of high-achieving students, role models, extracurricular involvement, inclusion of women as a topic in the curriculum, and recognition of the social realities facing women in the "real world." Essential elements seen in universities serving women students is visionary leadership committed to the education of women, a belief in women's capacities with high expectations, creating places for women's voices to be heard, providing opportunities for women's leadership, celebrating institutional history, and an active alumnae association.

Some scholars up until modern times argued that such institutions have advantages for young women over coeducation colleges, including in the areas of self-esteem building and curricula better tied to practical careers (Adler, 1994). A number of studies find students more satisfied with the experience at women's colleges, citing the fostering of leadership qualities that lead to greater career accomplishments. Additional characteristics of women's colleges touted are the positive role models of accomplished women in administrative leadership, and faculty across the disciplines including in the hard sciences. Finally, the all-female class is said to encourage more active participation in discussions (Tidball, Smith, Tidball, & Wolf-Wendel, 1999).

The most consistent criticism of women's colleges is that they give students an unrealistic view of the world because of their isolation. Advocates of women colleges argue that the best environment is one that prepares students for reality in a removed environment, while providing a quality education (Tidball, Smith, Tidball, & Wolf-Wendel, 1999). Some scholars have pointed to the complexity of the history and debate about women's colleges from their origin up until the present time. Bank notes, "Unlike the education of their male counterparts, women's higher education is enmeshed in a long tradition of gender-related contradictions and controversies" (2003, p.1).

Notions of gender traditionalism versus emancipation are at the heart of the complex attitudes regarding women's colleges. One such contradiction/ complexity is that women's colleges have been attacked as traditional, anachronistic, irrelevant, and overly protective of women, yet at the same time some defend these institutions as more emancipatory and less gender traditional than coeducational institutions.

Another complexity of women's colleges is that of the conflict in curricular emphasis on careerism versus a liberal arts education. This is a long debate in higher education generally, but one that has a specific gender bias at its root for women. As shown in the first and second chapters, women have generally pursued liberal arts more than men in the past up until the present.

For example, going back to the early 20th century, President Charles Van Hise of the University of Wisconsin argued that the tactic of "natural segregation" of men from women in coeducational college studies was a positive approach, with professional colleges of engineering, business and law as male sections of the university, and domestic sciences and nursing as those for women. At the end of the 20th century, one noted study found that undergraduate women attending Stanford University were considerably more likely than men to endorse a liberal education over careerist values (Katchadourian & Boli, 1985).

The reality is that despite the long argument over liberal education, even elite liberal arts institutions have made accommodations to careerism, sometimes through direct corporate-to-college linkages. The impact of a primarily liberal arts curriculum on women has been seen as detrimental by some. Mervin Freedman's (1961) study of Vassar College students revealed that those graduates who concentrated on a liberal arts education experienced greater conflict between their intellectual paths and eventual marriage, as opposed to those with careerist interests. He reasoned that "the emphasis in our society is, in short, on doing, not being; and unfortunately, the doing involved in being a wife and mother often brings little recognition, no matter how demanding the tasks involved, no matter how creative the participation" (pp. 26–27).

Some scholars point to the large number of women scientists produced by women's colleges, while others claim that such success is a result of elite status, not the fact that they admit only women. When women's colleges are compared to similar level coeducational institutions, women are equally successful (Faragher, 1988).

Sororities gave rise to some of the same contradictions as women's colleges—lauded as emancipatory venues for developing leadership skills and strong bonds among women, while at the same time attacked as elitist and conservative. Students entering sororities could expect to find a culture where most members valued marriage and family for themselves, while holding a belief in gender equality. Scholarly writing about women's colleges generally talks about them as being both gender traditional and emancipatory, while sororities are often spoken about in terms of an either/or debate and value.

Palmieri (1995) contends that critics who claim women's colleges lack feminism fail to see the significance of the shared women's intellectual power and mission which promoted a form of feminism. Women's colleges form a professional life for women, one that does not just mimic men, and importantly practice a critical feminist pedagogy. The innovative pedagogical approaches used at many women's colleges focus not on rote memorization, but instead on discussions, seminars, field trips, and laboratory work (see Chapter 6). In many ways women's colleges clearly have been influential on coeducational institutions in terms of curriculum, student services, and the promotion of high-minded social and religious activism.

## CASE STUDIES

This section looks at four specific institutions, each of which reveal special approaches to serving women students. Scripps College provides an illustration of a later iteration of the liberal arts women's college, linked to a unique consortium of elite colleges in Southern California. Xavier University of Louisiana and Mt. Saint Mary's University represent two Catholic women's colleges which concentrate on low-income and ethnic minority students. In their desire to serve these populations, they demonstrate innovation in delivery of their educational programs by paying close attention to unique needs. This is unlike the other women's colleges which often had the luxury of serving affluent women who could afford full-time residential experiences. Finally, the New School presents the intriguing history of a high-level urban alternative college emphasizing continuing education and social activism serving primarily educated women in New York City.

### Scripps College

Pomona College was founded in 1881 as a high-quality coeducational institution located just east of Los Angeles. The pressure of too many women applicants in the early 20th century was apparently one motivation to start

Scripps women's college as part of the new Claremont College consortium (Horowitz, 1984). Plans for an expansion were funded by the wealthy benefactor Ellen Browning Scripps, who amassed a fortune in the newspaper business. Scripps purchased the land where the current campus lies, and gave initial funding of $500,000 to Pomona College to create the new institution. At the time of the establishment of Scripps College, there were few places for women-only higher education in California. The college opened in the fall of 1927 with 50 female students (Scripps College, 1931; Walker, 1952).

The idea of Scripps was said to be "cultural" rather than "vocational." Also, a stated belief in the importance of a nurturing environment required a residential institution. To emphasize the retreat-like feel of the campus, the charming Denison Library of Scripps College has inscribed over its door: "Knowledge comes but Wisdom lingers."

The curriculum at Scripps was intended to be "geared to the realities of life," but also to provide a training in the humanities, as was reportedly Ellen Browning Scripps' wish: "Living is in itself the high art and she desired for women a college where the alphabet of this art might be mastered" (Walker, 1952, p. 32). Early leaders of the institution argued for an academically rigorous curriculum:

> Any development of curriculum which does not take into consideration the long struggle of women (covering at least twenty-six hundred years) for an opportunity to receive a liberal education identical with that available to men, is fundamentally unsound. In other words, truth must be presented to women as truth, not as truth adapted to women. In view of the presented position of women, any adaptation of general education to preconceptions of women's interests or intelligence is unfortunate, especially in a college the primary purpose of which is to prepare women to take a dignified place in the common enterprise of public life. (Scripps College, 1934, note #5)

In initial documents for the college, anti-mass education rhetoric was used, calling large coeducational universities "packing houses" where "campuses swarm with amorphous masses" in contrast to the small and personalized Scripps College. At these growing coeducational public institutions in the early 1930s it was said that "culture you could see distributed before your eyes somewhat the way ground coffee is poured into the waiting cans" (Scripps College, 1931, p. 22). "Here in Scripps College are fortified with the nourishment of centuries. Here their wakening sensibilities are converted into clear swift acts and thoughts. It is hoped that they will go forth a more vivid humanity, to stand free on the summits with whole rampant worlds enslaved" (p. 23).

Nevertheless, from the start Scripps College gave the students opportunity for coeducation by being allowed to take courses with male students at nearby Pomona College. Early documents of enrollment show almost one hundred courses taken by women students at linked Pomona College in a school year, while men from Pomona College took 29 courses at Scripps College (Scripps College, nd).

As a West Coast "Ivy," Scripps College is representative of the more elite women's colleges with a strong liberal education curriculum. Additionally, it reveals a women's college adjusting to the times, sometimes begrudgingly, by allowing coeducational classrooms, and by the end of the 20th century expanding the curriculum into the sciences, different teaching methods, and at the same time embracing Women's Studies as a discipline in its own right.

## Xavier University of Louisiana

According to university documents, Xavier University of Louisiana was founded by Katharine Drexel and the Sisters of the Blessed Sacrament as a Catholic and historically Black college. Founder Katharine Drexel was proclaimed a saint in the year 2000 for her work with disadvantaged African American and Native American people, the second American-born saint in the Catholic Church. Drexel was introduced to higher education when she attended the Catholic University of America in Washington, DC in a special summer session program. Catholic University was created to help nuns attain degrees and certificates needed to be effective teachers, an aim consistent with what would become Xavier University in Louisiana.

As with Mount Saint Mary's University, Xavier University is a Catholic women's college that focused from the start on lower-class and ethnic minority students. Xavier's mission was to "carry on the glorious work of extending the kingdom of Christ in the souls of Colored men and women" (Hughes, 2014, p. 131). Drexel's social activism paralleled that of the church which recognized the Indian problem evidenced by the establishment of the Catholic Commission for Indian Affairs in 1879. Drexel founded the Sisters of the Blessed Sacrament for Indians and Colored People in 1891, one of 134 orders of Catholic women founded in the United States.

The institution describes its purpose as to "contribute to the promotion of a more just and humane society by preparing its students to assume roles of leadership and service in a global society." In 1925 a Teachers College and College of Arts and Sciences had been established, and by 1927 a College of Pharmacy was added. A high school and a number of elementary schools staffed by the college in New Orleans created an educational ladder reaching from kindergarten through college. The university also awards the M.Th. in Theology through its Institute for Black Catholic Studies.

The university's major academic units are the College of Arts and the College of Pharmacy. Enrollment is now 69.7% African American and 26% Catholic. From the beginning, the administration, staff and faculty were diverse, including black, white, religious, and lay (Xavier University of Loui-

siana, 2019). The impact of Xavier on the local community has been significant, with 40% of public school teachers in New Orleans and four out of six
high school principals being graduates of the college (Hughes, 2014).

## Mount Saint Mary's University

Established by the Sisters of St. Joseph of Carondelet in 1925, Mount Saint
Mary's University states that it welcomes students of all faiths, nurturing
them in their intellectual and spiritual growth. As a Roman Catholic institution, the Mount is part of one of the oldest university traditions in the world.
The fleur-de-lis symbol of France in the College's academic seal represents
the sisters who trace their roots to Le Puy, France.

The university's first president was Mother Margaret Mary Brady who
was the province's superior in 1925, and responded to Bishop Cantwell's
request to establish a Catholic women's college in Los Angeles. At the time
of its founding, Mount St. Mary's was housed temporarily at St. Mary's
Academy, but two years later in 1928, the Sisters purchased 36 acres for a
new site stretched along the foothills of the Santa Monica mountains overlooking Los Angeles, now adjacent to the Getty Center.

The 1946–47 catalogue describes the college's mission: "The aim of
Mount St. Mary's College is to offer its students an instructional program in
the liberal arts that is Christian in its tradition and Catholic in its philosophy.
Through the educational program the college endeavors to develop the student's whole personality—intellectually, spiritually, socially, and physically"
(McNeil, 1985, p. 74). The college graduated its first students in 1929 at the
new campus.

In 1962, the university expanded to its second campus on the Doheny
Estate near downtown Los Angeles, designed to complement the educational
opportunities of the original Chalon Campus in West Los Angeles. The institution then began to offer innovative new programs, including graduate programs, a "Weekend College" for working adults who wanted to earn a baccalaureate degree, a two-year associate in arts program, and certificate programs.

The curriculum first focused on teaching and health sciences professions,
but expanded into the liberal arts. "In addition to emphasizing those branches
of knowledge which give the richest and most complete view of truth, and
which impart the cultural background for worthy leisure-time pursuits,
Mount St. Mary's offers a vocational program designed to prepare its students for those areas of service most in harmony with Christian womanhood"
(McNeil, 1985, p. 116). Notably, in the spring of 1953, Mount St. Mary's
began a program entitled "Every Woman's World," a lecture series on the
philosophy of the home, goals of homemaking, fashion, interior decorating,

the child, trends in foods, home appliances, landscape architecture, and the psychology of the home. It successfully ran for 10 years (McNeil, 1985).

Since its founding, the university has graduated more than 17,000 students, and the current student body is approximately 2,900. The university advises potential students that women's colleges are known for providing an educational environment that both nurtures and challenges women to be their best, that it is dedicated to helping students develop their talents, no matter what their area of academic interest.

The university cites statistics claiming that graduates of a women's college are twice as likely as female graduates of coeducational colleges and universities to earn a doctoral degree and attend medical school (59% of baccalaureate graduates from Mount Saint Mary's University go on to earn advanced degrees). The college claims that students who attend women's colleges report a higher degree of satisfaction with their college experience and in their interactions with faculty members (Mount Saint Mary's University, 2019a).

Women now make up 80% of the Mount faculty, a majority of the President's Cabinet, and half of the Board of Trustees. Finally, the Center for the Advancement of Women at Mount Saint Mary's University is a hub for gender equity research, advocacy, and leadership development. Its stated vision is to find solutions to persistent gender inequities and work with partners to eradicate them in our lifetime, and produces an annual report on the status of women in California. The 2019 document notes: "The Report also emphasizes the differences among women rather than comparing men and women broadly as we have done in the past" (Mount Saint Mary's University, 2019b, p. 3). The report highlights the complexity of identity for women:

> The idea that we find ourselves at the intersection of many identities that may have different relationships to power, privilege, oppression, and marginalization. All women, then, cannot simply be gathered under one label—"woman"—with the assumption that the experience of womanhood is common for us all. Rather, overlapping social-group identities (i.e., race, class, sexual orientation, immigration status, etc.) shape the experiences of anyone who identifies as a woman as much as being a woman shapes her participation in those other social groups. Further, the relationship of power and privilege comes into play both inside and outside of each social-group identity.

In the fall of 2017, women accounted for 2,926 out of 3,226 students, with 60% Hispanic. The graduation rate was 66% for women, and 68% for Hispanic students. Faculty salaries were the same for men and women (IPEDS, 2019).

**The New School**

Founded in 1919, the New School for Social Research, now named the New School, was started by a group of prominent intellectuals and educators including Charles Beard, John Dewey, James Harvey Robinson, and Thorstein Veblen. The New School arose out of controversy at Columbia University when two faculty were fired for expressing their opposition to American involvement in World War I. The Columbia president at the time argued that "academic freedom" for faculty was limited to a choice of research concentration, not political expression. In this way the emergent institution in 1918 was first organized by dissident academics from Columbia associated with the New Republic and social activists from the Women's Suffrage Movement, wanting an alternative to conventional university education that could be a self-governing community of scholars focused on social science aimed at reconstructing society along more egalitarian and scientific lines (Rutkoff & Scott, 1986).

The educational philosophy was influenced greatly by John Dewey and Thorstein Veblen, who were founders and teaching faculty. Veblen was a member of the original faculty the same year he published his *Higher Learning in America*. Dewey taught regularly through the 1940s, as well as served on institutional advisory boards. He insisted that learning should be across the lifespan, and saw this as a moral necessity. As he wrote in *Democracy and Education*, "Conscious life is a continual beginning afresh." The New School's initial focus was on adult education, which the founders felt was underdeveloped in America.

Veblen contended that the mixing of research and undergraduate instruction worked against the benefit of both. The size of universities thwarted close dialogue between faculty and students, and at the same time scholars wasted time managing classrooms instead of doing research. As a result, the New School at the graduate level focused on research rather than teaching. At the extension level, the founders saw adult education as a kind of apprenticeship. An informal teaching and family community atmosphere became the well-known style of the institution (Rutkoff & Scott, 1986).

The New School came to embody the informal, rebellious, bohemian world of Greenwich Village prior to World War II. It's emphasis on art, social reform, political radicalism, and disregard for convention fit within the developing Village in New York City. One of the most striking features from the beginning was the participation of women at the New School. Two thirds of the students were female.

A major shift at the New School came in 1933 as it became a "University in Exile" for those scholars escaping Hitler and Mussolini. From 1933 to 1944 the New School received 178 exiled scholars, more than any other American institution. The University in Exile was renamed the Graduate

Faculty in 1935, and over the years many important 20th century concepts came out of the school, including totalitarianism, the theory of conspicuous consumption, cultural pluralism, structuralism, gestalt psychology, business cycle theory, phenomenology, and happenings (Rutkoff & Scott, 1986).

After WWII, the New School grew from 1,300 to 4,500 students in the adult school. Women continued to outnumber men 2 to 1. The flexible curriculum was thought to be attractive to those women at the time reassessing their careers and new post-war opportunities. In addition, 25 to 30% of the students were Jewish, and the school had prominent New York City Jews on the board of directors. Discrimination against Jews in elite college admissions created a demand for a higher education alternative in New York City (Rutkoff & Scott, 1986).

The school became known for a "respectable radicalism" that attracted union leaders and social change groups for many years. The original goal was to create a new kind of academic institution to address the problems facing societies in the 20th century. The vision was to bring together scholars and citizens interested in questioning, debating, and discussing the most important issues of the day. The New School in the 1930s and 1940s became a significant research center for social science, and developed the first *Encyclopedia of Social Sciences*. The university grew to include five colleges, including the disciplines of social sciences, international affairs, liberal arts, history, and philosophy, as well as art, design, management, and the performing arts (Rutkoff & Scott, 1986).

The scheduling of classes in the late afternoon and evening allowed the school to draw on high quality faculty from around the Manhattan area to teach on overload. This approach reduced the New School's costs, and attracted exceptional faculty. Faculty members and visiting scholars included Harold Laski, Franz Boas, and John Maynard Keynes. In the late 1940s, Karen Horney and Erich Fromm introduced their new approaches to psychoanalysis. From 1954 to 1978, Margaret Mead taught courses in anthropology. In 1962, Gerda Lerner offered the first university-level course in women's history (Rutkoff & Scott, 1986).

The New School also became known for courses in the creative arts taught by innovative 20th-century artists, including Martha Graham, Frank Lloyd Wright, Aaron Copland, and W. H. Auden. In 1926, the school became the first American university to teach the history of film, and it was one of the first to offer college-level courses in photography and jazz (New School, 2019).

The mission of the New School today is stated thus:

> The New School prepares students to understand, contribute to, and succeed in a rapidly changing society, and thus make the world a better and more just place. We will ensure that our students develop both the skills a sound liberal

arts education provides and the competencies essential for success and leadership in the emerging creative economy. We will also lead in generating practical and theoretical knowledge that enables people to better understand our world and improve conditions for local and global communities.

According to its strategic plan, the institutional commitment is to social justice and now additionally sustainability (New School, 2014). In the Fall of 2017, there were 7,431 women of 10,389 total students. The graduation rate is high for women, at 71%, compared to 59% for men (2011 cohort) (IPEDS, 2019). The New School demonstrates the important link between women's higher education and continuing education.

## CONCLUSION

In this chapter, the history and development of women's and coeducational colleges were examined to better understand the background of the increase of female students in American colleges. Individual college profiles emphasize the great variety of institutional types in America serving different female populations, from the elite West Coast women's college, to Catholic women's colleges focused on ethnic minorities, and a unique urban school providing a high-level intellectual continuing educational environment for female intellectuals and social activists.

The development and growth of women's and coeducational institutions in America reveals early dominance of men-only institutions in the early 19th century, rapidly overtaken by coeducational institutions, many of them land grant colleges. Throughout the 20th century, there was a slow decline in the number of male or female-exclusive colleges.

Although the lack of public interest today is clear, the debate over the advantages and disadvantages of women-only colleges persists. The center of the debate concentrates on the question of what sort of education best prepares women for the gendered challenges of the world experienced by adults in their specific cultures. Most universities worldwide are coeducational, yet women's colleges provide access for some women who would not be able to attend college. In some countries because of cultural/religious beliefs, women-only colleges are necessary. This is true of India and some Middle Eastern countries in particular—there are 2,500 in India alone (Renn, 2014).

Bank (2003) argues that despite the fact that women will experience more gender equality in college than is likely in the workplace or home, inequities remain, and therefore what is needed is a gender-conscious education that encourages women to move beyond male-dominated definitions of what constitutes rewarding employment and personal life. Female faculty and administrators queried also pointed to some of the advantages of women's colleges: "I am a product of a woman's college decades ago: the presence of female faculty in the classroom, the stronger focus of female students on careers, not just jobs; the absence of competing in the classroom were all strong motivators for focusing on current coursework and future careers." One respondent identified the strength of women's colleges as being in their liberal arts curriculum and approach: "Working for [a women's college] the lessons learned from the women's colleges were not necessarily because it was women, but because it was small and liberal arts."

Some respondents pointed to the major concern often cited about single-sex institutions as not providing sufficient experience to effectively enter the mixed gender world after college: "I suppose woman's colleges help women develop the skills to push back against the challenges women will face in the world—the problem is that the world is gender diverse. Yes, of course, leadership opportunities abound in all female colleges (no male competition), but functional society isn't solely female. Wouldn't this be just as bad as an all-white college? Safety? . . . Are women really so weak that they cannot succeed in a diverse environment?"

One important legacy seen in tracing the history of women's colleges is the influence exerted on higher education as a whole to produce graduates with a civic consciousness. Women's colleges often had strong social activist and religious missionary types of purpose that encouraged women to be active in changing their communities for the better. This clear purpose made these early women's colleges stand out from men-only and coeducation institutions which often had more career-oriented purposes.

The profile of the two Catholic Colleges reveal how specific institutions have innovated in approaches to better serve low-income and ethnic minority female students. The unique New School presents the importance of informal and continuing education in creating an intellectual community of primarily women. The fifth chapter expands on the importance of informal ways of learning for women and reviews the history of forms of continuing education, salons, reading circles, as well as the importance of reading and writing in the collective intellectual development of women.

The next chapter turns its attention to a specific examination of women in college athletics. The landmark public policy shift in America resulting from Title IX implementation in 1972 is described, along with the large impact not only on women's sports but campus climate as well.

## DISCUSSION QUESTIONS

1. What are the strengths and weaknesses of women's colleges in serving female students?
2. How are Catholic colleges different from the Seven Sister institutions that they initially emulated?

3. What have been the primary challenges of coeducational institutions in serving a mixed student body?
4. Describe the process of elite colleges moving from male-only, to coordinate or linked colleges, to coeducational institutions.
5. What is particularly striking in the case studies of colleges presented in this chapter?

*Chapter Four*

# Women's Athletics in College and the Impact of Title IX

I began to watch women's college sports after buying an alumni membership at the University of California Los Angeles (UCLA), which allowed access to all "Olympic Sports"—meaning everything but football and men's basketball. UCLA has a proud college athletics history, winning more NCAA championships in all sports than any other university in America.

The institution also has a long record of promoting ethnic diversity in athletics, and notably was the college where Jackie Robinson lettered in four sports before going on to become the first African American player in previously segregated major league baseball. Although I had sporadically watched women's sports on television, and even joined pickup basketball games on occasion with female players, I was astonished by the athletes at UCLA. Even more notable than their skills and discipline was their evident comradery and competitiveness.

Indeed, watching these young women, who often seem to embody the highest ideals we hold as a society about athletes, led me to write this book. I can't help but wonder how much the rapid growth of women's college athletics has positively influenced changes throughout the university.

In the contempory history of women in higher education, the growth of women's athletics as a result of Title IX legislation is a significant thread. Although we will see that women's college athletics has appeared separate and distinct from the feminist movement, it is hard to minimize the empowering impact of large-scale participation of women in college athletics on the development of self-assured individuals, groups, and the overall campus culture.

*Chapter 4*

## HISTORICAL CONTEXT

Sports today harken back to the public displays and rituals of ancient Greece and Italy. According to Potter (2012), there is a direct link between the ancient and the modern world of athletics. The crucial feature of sports is that it enables those outside the arena to feel linked with those within, and empowered. Novak (1994) argues that athletics meet a deep natural impulse that is "radically religious," fulfilling an impulse for freedom, ritual, symbolic meaning, and perfection. In this way sports are a form of religion and even godliness.

Gender differentiation in athletics may have occurred in part because of a link between sport and preparation for war. The Duke of Wellington allegedly credited the victory of English forces at Waterloo to the playing fields of Eton (Fields, 2008). Physical skills have traditionally been defined by male characteristics. Ellis (2014) argues that perhaps if athletics had been shaped by women instead of men, balance, flexibility, and ultra-endurance might replace faster, higher, and stronger as valued physical skills in athletics (Ellis, 2014).

**Figure 4.1. Women's Rowing Team, Potomac Boat Club (1919).** *National Photo Company Collection (Library of Congress).*

Looked at historically, the association in America of sports with religion and manhood is a consistent theme. Carl Case in *The Masculine in Religion* (1906) argued that the church had grown overly passive and feminine, and was becoming to his horror a place that seemed natural for women, and unnatural for men. Alarmed by the prospect of overcivilized middle- and upper-class managerial types being toppled by lower-class workers and muscular immigrants, many Progressive Era (1890–1920) reformers endorsed exercise and outdoor activities such as hiking and camping as a remedy.

This prevailing attitude led in 19th-century America to the idea of "Muscular Christianity" (Ellis, 2014). According to Putney (2001), the notion of Muscular Christianity had prominent supporters such as G. Stanley Hall, the first President of the American Psychological Association, and President Theodore Roosevelt, who advocated for the related concept of "the Strenuous Life." Theodore Roosevelt's personal story was that of an asthmatic child raised in a wealthy New York family, who eventually remade himself into the very image of American masculinity, emphasizing vigor, action over reflection, experience over book learning, and pragmatic idealism. The emergence of the YMCA, although founded in 1844 in London, quickly grew into an important American organization propagating notions of Muscular Christianity.

Gender segregation in athletics was justified in early America by the supposed need for a masculine preserve, a space in which boys could learn to become men away from the "interference" of their mothers (Starr & Brant, 1999). Conversely, athletics for women had to be justified as a means of enhancing physical beauty and reproductive capacity. Women were encouraged to be involved in healthy exercise, but only up to a point. For females, the argument was that pleasure and recreation should be the focus instead of strenuous training or competition.

Warnings about women exercising too much were common in the late 19th century, with claims it would lead to so called "muscle molls" and lesbianism. For example, Dudley Allen Sargent from Harvard famously argued that female competitors tended to become too masculine, and forecast an ominous future when effeminate men would succumb to overly virile women (Ellis, 2014). Consequently, most of the early concentration for women athletics programs in schools and college in America was on physical education, rather than competitive sports. The Boston Normal School established in 1889 was an early example of a physical education program dedicated to building female strength without the competitive sports facet.

Women's basketball at the college level was one of the first areas where progress was made in female competitive sports. Invented by Canadian James Naismith in a YMCA gym class, basketball was an indoor game and considered not as rough as football—therefore more appropriate for women (Grundy & Shackelford, 2005). The first college women's basketball game

**Figure 4.2.   1913–1914 basketball game, no. 38, Vassar College, May (1913).**
*Wolven, E. L., photographer (Library of Congress).*

was held on April 4, 1896, with Stanford playing Berkeley. It drew great interest from the public with extensive newspaper coverage, and attracted seven hundred spectators.

In the 20th century, high-profile female athletes such as Olympian "Babe" Didrikson brought women's sports to the national forefront, but also caused some subsequent push back with negative characterizations of such celebrities as appearing suspiciously homosexual. In order to counter this public apprehension, the Amateur Athletic Union (AAU) in 1954 conducted a study called "Statistical Survey of Former Women Athletes" which demonstrated from a survey that 91% were married and 79% had children—apparently indicating that these athletes were certified heterosexuals.

Changes in attitudes toward women's athletics were slow to come in the 20th century until a revolution started with the passage of Title IX, the Education Amendment Act of 1972. The act required all educational programs and student activities to be treated on an equal basis between the sexes, requiring that women's athletic programs receive the same (or equivalent) services and benefits as those available to men's programs. Farchmin (2003) notes that one of the fascinating aspects of Title IX's passage was the lack of understanding by many at first of the coming impact on college athletics.

The National Collegiate Athletic Association (NCAA) did not initially see Title IX as a threat because of bigger issues they faced with declining financial support for men's athletics during the economic recession (Belanger, 2016). However, the NCAA eventually came to appreciate Title IX's threat to the status quo, and in the early 1970s put $1 million toward lobbying efforts. In May 1974 Senator John Tower proposed that football, and other revenue-producing sports, be excluded from Title IX coverage. The resulting Tower Amendment was later overturned by the congressional committee charged with reviewing Title IX's specific regulations (Farchmin, 2003). There was then an extended period of legal complaints filed between 1975 and 1980 over the implementation of Title IX as colleges tried to navigate the new legal landscape (Belanger, 2016).

Women's athletic programs were closely tied to academic departments, while men's sports, especially at the large universities, were often commercialized and disconnected from the educational mission of the university. As a result, faculty in physical education played a much stronger role in women's athletics than in male sports, which led to consistently different outcomes for the student athletes and divergent implementation of Title IX (Belanger, 2016).

There were generally two competing expressed purposes for college athletics: student self-development or university revenue production. Women's sports were viewed exclusively within the self-development context (Hoffman, Iverson, Allan & Ropers-Huilman, 2010). It is important to keep this notion in mind when considering the statistical variance considered later in this chapter concerning the impact of college athletics on students, which seems to be more positive for women than men.

One important part of the story of the development of women's college athletics is the formation of the Association for Intercollegiate Athletics for Women (AIAW) in 1971 to govern collegiate women's sports in the United States, and to administer national championships. As this new association developed just in advance of Title IX, it navigated a course separate from male collegiate athletics, one consistent with the historical roots of women's sports in academic departments. The AIAW presidents faced constant conflict during their association's brief existence (1971–82), but their most formidable crisis was the threat of the NCAA taking over women's athletic programs altogether. Indeed, once the NCAA lost the legislative battles over Title IX, it worked to get rid of the AIAW (Wilson, 2013).

The two organizations had distinct origins, with the NCAA formed primarily to clean up problems in men's college athletics, whereas the AIAW was created to enact an idealistic and radically student-centered model of intercollegiate sport. One main controversy for the AIAW was its opposition to scholarships for athletes and its prohibiting scholarship awardees from participating in association events. The AIAW leadership saw scholarships and aggressive recruiting as incompatible with the educational model for which they advocated (Belanger, 2016).

President Reagan's administration attempted to dampen enforcement of Title IX, and in 1984 the Supreme Court ruled that Title IX did not necessarily apply to athletics. Nevertheless, in 1988 the picture brightened at the federal level when Congress passed the Civil Rights Restoration Act to reinstate mandates struck down by the Supreme Court, explicitly stating that all school-sponsored programs, athletics included, must live up to Title IX edicts. Furthermore, in 1992 the Supreme Court ruled that a victim of sex bias under Title IX could sue for monetary damages, putting financial teeth into the measure. The NCAA has continued up to the present day to try to exempt high-revenue football and basketball from enforcement of Title IX without luck (Belanger, 2016).

## INCREASED PARTICIPATION IN SPORTS

Although the Fourteenth Amendment was adopted in 1868, only after Title IX was enacted more than a hundred years later did the courts conclude that the equal protection clause allowed young women equal access to sports. It was up to the Fourteenth Amendment to provide the practical legal force for Title IX. The Javits Amendment was adopted instead of the Tower Amendment, which instructed the Department of Health, Education, and Welfare (HEW) to create a provision in the regulations that would include, with respect to intercollegiate athletic activities, reasonable provisions based on the nature of the particular sports. The amendment thus asked to protect male collegiate sports from women, especially in football.

As a result, HEW chose to distinguish between contact and noncontact sports. Title IX made one important exclusion that members must be allowed to try out for sports "unless the sport involved is a contact sport." Contact sports were defined as "boxing, wrestling, rugby, ice hockey, football, basketball and other sports the purpose or major activity of which involved bodily contact." The complexity of America's relationship to boxing in general, and female boxers in particular, stems in part from the paradoxes of boxing as being historically a racial battlefield (Fields, 2008).

There was an immediately positive impact on female participation in sports as a result of Title IX. During the 1970–71 academic year, before Title IX, high school girls composed just 7% of the pool of athletes, while in 1972–73, immediately after Title IX was enacted, those numbers rose to 17% for young women. In 1970, prior to the 1972 enactment of Title IX, there were only 2.5 women's teams per school and a total of only about 16,000 female intercollegiate athletes (Figure 4.3). In 2014, forty-two years after the enactment of Title IX, there was an average of 8.83 women's teams per school and over 200,000 female intercollegiate athletes (Acosta & Carpenter, 2015).

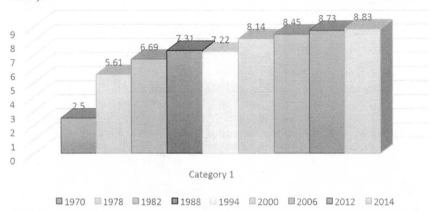

Category 1

■1970 ▦1978 ▦1982 ■1988 ▢1994 ▦2000 ▦2006 ■2012 ▦2014

**Figure 4.3.    Average # of Women's Varsity Teams per School. *Acosta & Carpenter, 2015.***

The public soon realized the importance of Title IX as evidenced by *Sports Illustrated* naming 1974 the Year of the Woman in Sports (Gilbert & Williamson, 1974). The impact of this policy change at the end of the 20th century grew year by year, and was highlighted by the American women's soccer team winning the 1999 World Cup. *Newsweek* reported that "World Cup Fever seemed to signal that twenty-seven years after Title IX legislation mandated equal financing for girls' athletics, women's team sports have truly arrived."

While basketball has been the success story of female forays into traditionally male American games, soccer captured media attention to the point that the House of Representatives debated whether a congratulation resolution should refer to Title IX after the 1999 World Cup victory (Fields, 2008). The 2019 World Cup victory by American women cemented the influence of Title IX on women's sports, and furthermore gave the athletes a platform for pointing out compensation inequality in professional athletics.

## ACADEMIC AND CAREER OUTCOMES

Evidence of the positive influence of participation in college athletics, while uneven for men, is clear for women. The NCAA commissioned Gallup (2016) to interview 1,670 former NCAA student athletes about their college experiences and current well-being, and compared the responses to those of nearly 23,000 non–student athletes graduating from the same colleges. The findings revealed that former student athletes rated higher than other college graduates in four out of the five elements of post-collegiate well-being. Among student athletes, women stood out versus non–student athletes in employment rates and workplace engagement. The report defines engagement as

> people more involved in and enthusiastic about their work. They are loyal and productive. Those who are not engaged may be productive and satisfied with their workplaces, but they are not intellectually and emotionally connected to them. Workers who are actively disengaged are physically present but intellectually and emotionally disconnected. They are unhappy with their work, share their unhappiness with their colleagues and are likely to jeopardize the performance of their teams. (Gallup, 2016, p. 9)

In Figure 4.4, one can see that former female student athletes excel in this category of engagement.

Former student athletes also felt more connected to faculty members while in college and participated in more extracurricular activities, and outperformed other college graduates on important career and life outcomes as well. They were significantly more likely to be engaged in their work and thrived in several areas of well-being compared with other college graduates—including their male former student athlete counterparts. When it comes to the likelihood of having a great job, female former student athletes win across the board on these comparisons (Gallup, 2016). Additionally, in another study, female executives reported participation in sport helps accelerate leadership and career potential: global research reveals that executive

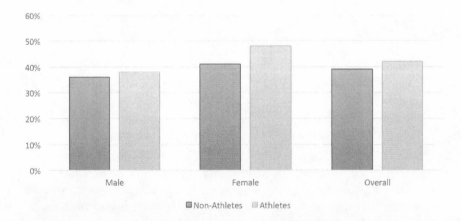

**Figure 4.4.   Student Engagement Comparison.** *Gallup, 2016.*

women are more likely to have played a sport and to hire other women who have played (Female Executives, 2014).

Some scholars have focused on life skills that are learned through competition, and often found in female athletes. Niendorf (2007) explored those positive attributes such as competitiveness, hard work, leadership, self-motivation, teamwork, time management, communication, confidence, and role modeling that college women athletes transferred to other areas of their lives. McKinney (2007) investigated the impact of partaking in athletics on women's academic experience at three select Jesuit colleges and universities with National Collegiate Athletic Association (NCAA) Division I programs. The conclusion was clear: athletes from the three institutions felt the presence of care and support as student athletes competing at the NCAA Division I level. Similarly, at the high school level, Hanson and Kraus (1998) discovered that young women's involvement in high school sports often has a strong and positive association with their success in science in their sophomore and senior years of high school.

Research on the impact of college athletics on males is less encouraging. Lindo, Swenson and Waddell (2011) considered the relationship between collegiate football success and non-athlete student performance, finding that the team's success significantly reduces male grades relative to female grades. Using survey data, they saw that males are more likely than females to increase alcohol consumption, decrease studying, and increase partying in response to the success of the team.

Jackovic (1999) investigated nine outcomes associated with the overall college experience for male athletes at an NCAA Division I university. The nine outcomes investigated included overall college satisfaction, overall college success, and Arthur Chickering's seven student development outcomes. The researcher found important differences among revenue, non-revenue, and club sport athletes in terms of their perceptions of how their college athletic experience impacted their overall college satisfaction, college success, and student development.

## CRITICAL PERSPECTIVES

Analysis of women in college sports concentrates on the intersection of race, lack of female coaches, and absorption into male athletic traditions. Some researchers (Hoffman, Iverson, Allan, & Ropers-Huilman, 2010) argue for the importance of race and class consideration in understanding the context of gains by women, because females of color have largely not benefited from athletic opportunities in the same way as white women. In general, noticeably absent from intercollegiate athletics research is the experience at Historically Black Colleges and Universities (HBCUs) (Cooper, 2013; Gawrysiak, Cooper, & Hawkins, 2013).

One of the consistent issues that arises in the research literature on women's athletics is the lack of female coaches. After Title IX and the merging of men's and women's athletic departments, women's sports became more attractive to male coaches due to higher salaries and an elevated status. Men rushed into these new coaching positions and the occupation became dominated by men. Ironically, Title IX seems to have had an "affirmative action for men" effect (La Croix, 2007). Despite an increase in women's athletic programs and subsequently the number of coaching positions available, more men than women filled these new positions.

Thus, the occupation of coach for women's sports shifted from one dominated by women in the early 1970s (when over 90% of coaches of women's sports were women) to one dominated by men in 2004 (when 44% of coaches of women's sports were women) (Acosta & Carpenter, 2015). Some argue that it is typical to blame women for the lack of female coaches, rather than institutional bias (LaVoi, 2016). Since evidence suggests that the gender of the coach influences the interpersonal relationship an athlete develops with her coach, including the likelihood of her identifying her coach as a role model, the lack of female coaches may have a continuing negative impact on students (Dowhower, 2000).

Russell (2015) asks if Title IX implementation, resulting in dramatic increases in the number of women competing on American collegiate sports teams, has on balance positively impacted female athletes. Or instead, have women been forced to adopt the male model of collegiate competition? Would the increases in participation and the opportunities for female athletes, female coaches, and female administrators have been even more dramatic if the AIAW had survived? Perhaps the principles of education, participation, and character that governed women's athletics for nearly 100 years have been lost in a system that only sees one, more traditionally male way of administering athletics.

Some scholars (Coad, 2008; Ross, 2005) look at how gender roles in sports are changing and how social meanings and realities are constructed by present-day college women athletes with constraints on gender displays. McClung (1996) contends that participation in intercollegiate sports has the potential to provide an environment which sensitizes women athletes to the role of gender in society, while at the same time limiting athletes' awareness of women's issues and the development of a feminist consciousness. She notes that athletes' lack of understanding of and sensitivity to women's issues are apparent.

In her study, athletes recognized the secondary status of women in society and the discriminatory nature of sports, but did not see an impact of this status on their lives. Athletes tended to disassociate themselves from feminism and women's issues because of the perceived negative connotations associated with these terms. Discussions about women's issues rarely occurred with administrators and coaches. Athletes felt that discussions were limiting because of negative perceptions associated with feminism and women's issues. Sports were generally not perceived as an appropriate context for discussing women's issues.

## MEDIA REPRESENTATION

Historically, the "female athlete" was considered a deviant figure—especially a woman who played previously masculine team sports. Fischesser (2008) points out that articulating an identity as a woman and an athlete has been changing since the passage of Title IX. The phrase "Title IX" has taken on cultural force as a narrative about the increased institutionalization and incorporation of women's sports into the expanding global sports and media complex. As this has happened, women describe ambivalent ways they were drawn into the media as girls and the sexual identifications articulated about the "female athlete." In Fischesser's study, the strong connection to the group and the women's individual identification as a teammate isolated and protected them from some of the assumed deviance that has been associated with being a "female athlete."

Champion (2006) looked at how Title IX changed women's athletics from an educational, social, and athletic perspective. Attitudes toward women and the role they play in intercollegiate athletics departments are far different than they were prior to Title IX. The public perception of women in athletics has also changed.

Women are no longer relegated to only playing in the shadows of male athletes. The lawmakers and courts have had a major impact on many of the changes that have affected colleges and universities because of Title IX enforcement. As evinced by their decisions in recent years, the courts have remained consistent in their support of Title IX and in the application of the laws, which has impacted media representation.

One aspect of college athletics at the end of the 20th century up to the present time has been the importance it has played in creating television content. As television began to expand available channels beyond the big three networks, there was an increased demand for content. Live sporting events were a ready source of such material. Professional and big-time college sports programs today are often little more than television programs with a live audience. Even less popular women's sports are regularly now shown on television, especially the conference-specific cable channels.

Some research suggests that female athlete images prompt less self-objectification, suggesting the need for more of this imagery in mainstream media

(Daniels, 2009). But despite the steady increase in the volume of women's sport participation, female athletes continue to be underrepresented in the media overall because of prominence of placement or scheduling and visual representations (Sherry, Osborne, & Nicholson, 2016). Murray (2018) utilized a content analysis of *Sports Illustrated* covers from 1954–2016 to evaluate the amount and type of coverage permitted to female athletes and found that it differs in both quantity and quality in coverage afforded to female athletes compared to male athletes.

Researchers have focused on the difference between male and female sports fans. Though women's sports have seen an explosion of growth and popularity during the past decade, many women do not consider themselves fans of female sports (Farrell, 2006). While women are increasingly becoming invested fans of men's football, baseball, hockey, and basketball, the perceived barriers—sociological, psychological and practical—to watching women's sports still appear formidable for many female fans. Pope (2017) considered women's experiences of sports spectatorship in the contemporary period and contended that there are a variety of types of women sports fans—it is not a homogeneous group. Often women are strongly identified with place and civic pride in relation to sports.

## BEAUTY PAGEANTS

One example and symptom of the complex nature of women's role and image in universities, and how it has evolved over time, is to look at beauty pageants. Since the 1920s, at the height of the rise of women in college, beauty pageants were sponsored by universities. Physical attractiveness, charm, heterosexual desirability, poise, and popularity were key elements of the "beauty" that was celebrated in these collegiate competitions.

The pageants arose in part as a response to the scrutiny of women joining the academy: "A barrage of class-coded instructions and expectations for how to improve their bodies and cultivate feminine charm, heterosexual desirability, and respectability" (Tice, 2012). Etiquette books for college were common in the middle 20th century including *The Freshman Girl: A Guide to College Life* (1925), *Co-etiquette: Poise and Popularity for Every Girl* (1936), and *She's Off to College: A Girls' Guide to College* (1940). Popular magazines of the time, such as *Mademoiselle Magazine*, focused greatly on college life and model female behavior and fashion.

According to Tice (2012), modern women of that time began to understand self-display as part of social mobility. This made them more beholden to consumption, fashion, and body aesthetics. Beauty contests reassured those afraid of the upsurge of women in universities by bolstering traditional constructions of proper femininity and gender boundaries. The competitions were used to neutralize the threat of women on campus by emphasizing heterosexual and middle-class notions of femininity.

To this day, college beauty pageants are especially important at HBCUs because of the stereotypical characterizations of black women as deficient in femininity and oversexed. Originally, there was the feeling that black women needed to prove they were dignified and coded as middle class and virtuous. "Black queens frequently aspire to the campus throne as a strategy to challenge exclusivity and invisibility, to repair the damaging legacies of racism" (Tice, 2012, p. 101). Unlike at predominately white schools, rarely have beauty pageants at HBCUs met with criticism or protest, even in the 1960s, because of the context.

## CONCLUSION

Title IX is the tale of two different world views clashing. In the old view men ruled and played contact sports. In the new world after 1972, women wanted political power and access to all sports. The previous prohibition from sports was exclusion from power structures.

Although the opportunities for female athletes grew greatly in the post-Title IX era, compliance by the majority of colleges and universities is an ongoing struggle. Furthermore, Title IX complicated the economic conditions facing collegiate athletics, given that most programs run at deficits, and both men and women's athletics struggle for additional funding (Forman, 2001). Belanger (2016) argues for the need of discussion about the fair allocations of resources in collegiate athletics. Although there is improvement since 1974 when men's athletic budgets consumed a remarkable 98% of the college athletics budget, challenges remain.

Figure 4.5 shows that, on average, in no individual sport do women's athletics make a profit, and in men's sports only football and basketball end with revenue beyond expenses.

One large study (Randleman, 1997) concluded that female university administrators have a more favorable attitude toward intercollegiate athletic competition for women than do athletic directors. According to La Croix (2007), despite improved athletic opportunities for girls and women since passage of Title IX of the Educational Amendments of 1972, collegiate athletic budgets dedicated to women's sports are smaller than the percentage of women athletes, and women's representation as athletic administrators and coaches for women's sports has declined.

Title IX resulted in the majority of colleges merging their men's and women's athletic departments under the leadership of a single head athletic director, who is nearly universally a man. La Croix (2007) found that schools with proportionally more women athletic administrators and schools that

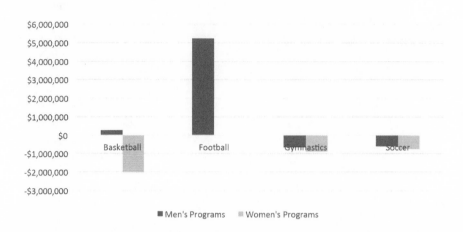

**Figure 4.5. Net Revenue Athletic Program Comparison. *NCAA, 2016.***

have relatively more women as head coaches of women's sports, pay lower average salaries to head coaches of women's sports, and dedicate relatively more of their operating budgets to women's sports. One can see from Figure 4.6 that coaches' salaries for men far exceed that of women.

The impact of Title IX legislation, and subsequent legal interpretations, has had a much larger influence on colleges than just on women's athletics. Many do not completely appreciate that Title IX forbids discrimination based on sex, not just in sports but all parts of federally funded education in America, including admissions and funded science research. In an April 2011 policy letter from the Department of Education, Title IX became a significant legal tool for addressing discrimination against students in the form of sexual harassment which sent universities scrambling to implement (Belanger, 2016).

Interestingly, although Title IX legislation arose in a political environment of feminist activism, that movement's relationship to the rise of collegiate women's athletics is problematic. Just as athletes were reluctant to embrace feminism or activism, feminist groups were slow to seek alliance with women who played sports. Many feminists saw sports, especially men's sports culture, as connected with all abhorrent in a patriarchal society that glorified competition, winning at all costs, and norms for masculinity rooted in misogyny, homophobia, and violence (Belanger, 2016).

Overall, while it is difficult to directly link every instance to the influence of Title IX on the overall rise of women on college campuses, the positive effect is evident. As one survey respondent for this book noted, "The increased participation of women in college sports has rippled out into other aspects of college life academically and culturally." Questions remain about

**Figure 4.6.   Total Salaries and Benefits Division 1.** *NCAA, 2016.*

how women's college athletics will further develop in the future. How will they be positioned in relationship to men's sports? Will advances in women's athletics become more clearly intertwined with other advances in the new type of university being created for an increasingly female student body?

The next chapter explores the significance of informal learning for women, and describes how through informal discussion, reading, and writing they became readied for advanced higher education when the doors finally pushed open.

## DISCUSSION QUESTIONS

1. Describe the historical context within which women's athletics developed in American colleges.
2. Describe the various ways that Title IX has impacted women students in relationship to athletics, academics, and campus climate.
3. What are the continuing challenges for women's sports programs at the collegiate level?
4. Describe the differences in approach between men's and women's college sports.
5. What was the significance of the Association of Intercollegiate Athletics for Women (AIAW)?

*Chapter Five*

# Learning Outside the Academy

Faced with formal exclusion from higher education, how were women with intellectual curiosity and a desire to express themselves to respond? They turned to reading, writing, and thoughtful discussion in a momentous way. In this chapter we detail an important part of the story of the rise of women in higher education: the way in which women through informal learning, reading, and writing prepared themselves for entrance into the male-only academy.

There has been much recent discussion about the fact that the majority of readers are women, as seen in articles such as "Are Boys the Weaker Sex?" by Anna Mulrine (2001) in the *U.S. News and World Report*. Only slightly more than one-third of adult American males now read literature (Figure 5.1).

In 2016, a Pew Research Center survey of adult reading habits concluded that "women are more likely to read books than men," and noted that 32% of men (versus only 23% of women) said that they hadn't read a single book in the past year. Overall, on average women read 15 books per year, compared to nine for men (Pew Research Center, 2016). Furthermore, this reading tendency starts at a young age. According to Scholastic's survey of over 2000 U.S. children ages 6–17, only 52% of boys (versus 72% of girls) said they liked reading books over the summer (Scholastic, 2019).

As women were generally restricted from formal higher education until the late 19th century, they instead developed intellectually through informal learning methods, most importantly through reading and writing. The reading and writing association with the socio-political upsurge of women and gaining access to education is crucial, but often overlooked. In this chapter the history of women outside the academy through reading, writing, and various forms of informal education is examined. In addition, women in college

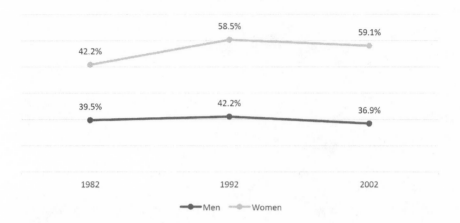

**Figure 5.1.    Literary Reading by Gender Trend. *NEA, 2002.***

novels and films are studied to better understand the cultural context and
public representations of this great social change.

## WOMEN READERS

While reading from the beginning of human civilization was a male domain,
this reality slowly changed over time. In Europe, Latin was associated with
men from aristocratic households, while vernacular language was connected
to females, and therefore less authoritative. There was a clear literacy distinction between the casual female language, which was thought of as passive
and obedient, and masculine expression characterized as socially valuable in
public discourse. In fact, the first four dictionaries of the English language
were explicitly aimed at explaining "hard words" to female readers (Ferguson, 2003).

Women often first read for religious purposes in accepted texts such as
the *Book of Hours* and various church primers of the times (Willard, 1984).
Lacking access to many formal educational opportunities, especially at the
advanced level, women have from early times turned to books as a source for
knowledge and human history. According to Manguel (2014), quoting Francisco de Quevedo from the 16th century, books function to eliminate barriers
of time and space, and allow "conversations with the dead." Up until the 17th
century when women were generally not allowed to own property, they did
own books, and tended to passed them along to their daughters, to set the
stage for continuing conversations with ancestors.

In this way books provided the informal education of women. Women
who learned to read in the 17th century were considered dangerous by many

**Figure 5.2. Women Reading in Normal School, Washington D.C. (1899).** *Johnston, Frances Benjamin, photographer (Library of Congress).*

men because they acquired a space to develop their own worldview, one that didn't necessarily correspond with that of male traditions (Fowler, 2005). As late as the early 19th century in Britain and North America it was still considered unseemly by some men for a female to be observed reading in public (Fischer, 2003).

In the 18th century with the development of capitalism and the industrialization of England, freed from many of their chores previously done in the home making products that were now available as manufactured goods, women experienced a great increase in leisure time. This free time led them to read, and spurred the development of the novel (Watt, 1957). Furthermore, capitalism brought about economic specialization and increased individual choice for both men and women. One scholar noted:

> The division of labor has done much to make the novel possible: partly because the more specialized the social and economic structure, the greater the number of significant differences of character, attitude and experience in con-

temporary life which the novelist can portray, and which are of interest to his
readers. (Watt, 1957, p. 71)

Some also claimed that the novel only arose as women gained importance
overall in society, and thus romantic relationships became important in society and in fiction. Previously, the legal position of women in the 18th century
was based on Roman law that affirmed only the head of the household as a
legal entity (Watt, 1957). The rise of the novel came about with the greater
freedom of women in modern society, especially regarding marriage, which
was achieved in England earlier than in the rest of the world.

Additionally, the development of a modern postal system in England
spurred written communication. Penny post starting in 1680 in London was
cheap, fast, and efficient. Women readers became targeted as an audience for
publications with emerging periodicals such as *Ladies Mercury* in 1693, *The
Female Tatler* (1709), and the *Female Spectator* (1744).

One additionally important development in the United Kingdom was the
creation of private lending libraries in which patrons could rent books for a
small fee. After 1740 lending libraries developed quickly, especially in London. Novels were the main attraction for patrons at these libraries, and led to
a quickly enlarged reading public, especially among the lower classes. Wom-
en servants specifically were one of the chief groups of lending library users,
and were ardent novel readers (Watt, 1957).

Reading also became a group activity for women. A clear predecessor of
English reading groups, and the growing intellectual activity of women, were
the French salons of the 18th century. While generally in Europe at that time
women had a very low social status, in Paris women led salons which they
developed and used to influence intellectual and cultural discussions. As one
scholar described the salons,

> The influence of women in the society of France before the Revolution is one
> of the interesting features of the eighteenth century. It was an influence which
> was paramount, paradoxically enough, when they made no pretension to politi-
> cal power or to literary reputation, and it was obtained, not in competing with
> men, or by the exercise of masculine gifts, but by a brilliant display of essen-
> tially feminine qualities united to mental superiority. (Clergue, 1907, p. 119)

The French salons were highly influential within France and in England and
were attended by all the great intellectuals of the time period, male and
female. The education of women was a regular topic at these gatherings
(Clergue, 1907).

For many women, reading was not only an individual pleasure, but a
group activity. In the 18th and 19th century in both England and America it
became commonplace for women to read together in their homes. These
early forms of reading circles, or book clubs, were a complex mix of piety,

self-improvement, irreverence, and social exchange that shaped society. The home and the tea table became part of the new informal world of knowledge exchange for women of the time.

In reaction, by the late 18th century there was opposition from some quarters to women reading novels, claiming that nations were becoming full of women addicted to the seductions of fiction. Women were thought to read differently than men and were prone to addiction, consumed by fantastical notions of love and gallantry, and prone to rapid identification with characters. Reading was said for some to have elicited alarmingly intense feelings in women. It was argued that if young women engaged in solitary compulsive reading of fiction, they were apt to have lascivious thoughts, and false expectations of what life was likely to offer them as adults (Williams, 2017).

In America, reading has long been an important vehicle for promoting and sustaining women's aspirations, and it had special resonance for young women in the years following the Civil War. According to the 1850 census, only 10 percent of the population over the age of 20 were unable to read and write, men and women in equal numbers. Reading allowed women to move beyond their everyday circumstances, and was one of the few generally tolerated female pleasures (Sicherman, 2010).

One of the most significant groups to structure formal reading groups in the United States was the Chautauqua Literary and Scientific Circle (CLSC). Of the 225,000 members in CLSC between 1878 and 1894, 80% were women. These reading circles were extremely popular in 19th-century America—by 1900 there were over 10,000 such groups, and they became an important instrument for the informal education of women outside of the academy. Influential women such as Jane Addams, often described as the mother of social work and first American Nobel Peace Prize winner, started reading circles. In Addams's case, her first choice for her circle was George Eliot's difficult and controversial *Romola* (1863).

Another key way that women in the 19th century could learn informally was through libraries. In fact, women became the main book borrowers from public libraries in America. For recent immigrant women, free lending libraries were an especially important way to learn English and become educated without the prohibitory cost of formal education. Given traditional restrictions on female literacy, Jewish women had special reason to believe in and support American access to books through libraries—they offered double freedom for them as women and Jews. Ironically, the cultural devaluation of female literacy allowed women greater access to secular learning than for men in Jewish culture.

By 1920, reading circles and other informal learning methods for women were slowly replaced to some extent by other cultural opportunities such as higher education and media, especially movies. Nevertheless, today reading groups such as Oprah's Book Club show the sustained interest by women in reading (Sicherman, 2010). Additionally, the use of libraries and participation in continuing education are consistently disproportionately female activities.

## EUROPEAN WOMEN WRITERS

In Europe by the 14th century women gradually became literate, especially young noblewomen and daughters of merchants who assisted their families with bookkeeping and correspondence. Christine de Pizan, Moderata Fonte,

**Figure 5.3.　Woman writing (1892).** *Phillips, John Edwin, photographer (Library of Congress).*

and Mary Wollstonecraft were three of the early European writers who had an important influence on subsequent women authors and thinkers. Christine de Pizan became attached to the French Royal Court, and many consider her an early champion of women's rights. She was raised in a bookish environment and inspired by both her father and her husband, but was essentially self-taught.

De Pizan became an expert notary for elite French society and was known for her distinctive handwriting. In her renowned *The Book of the City of Ladies* (1405) she wrote about creating an ideal city free of misogyny, and proudly listed accomplished women throughout history in traditionally male fields, arguing that if women went to the same schools as their brothers, their capabilities would undoubtedly be equal to men's. This book was one of the first to invoke the authority of a woman's own experience, and indeed she was one of the early known female professional writers (Bollmann, 2018).

Unknown before the 1980s, Moderata Fonte's 1592 dialogue, *The Merits of Women*, is now considered a classic of feminist thought. It vividly describes women's daily lives of the period and asserts women's worth. She wrote that "God never created any man (a man who was simply a man, that is) who could match that woman who was entirely a woman" (Fonte, 2018, p. 47).

Finally, the early woman writer who probably had the greatest influence on the public and the subsequent women's rights movement was Mary Wollstonecraft. Her 1792 work entitled *A Vindication of the Rights of Women* insisted on an important link between the French Revolution, and women's rights efforts generally. She claimed that both genders should be subject to the same laws and ethics.

Another Wollstonecraft essay, *Thoughts on the Education of Daughters*, disapproved of social practices such as baby talk, cosmetics, and other frivolity, and described the state of women as "unfortunate females who are left by inconsiderate parents to struggle with the world, and whose cultivation of mind renders the endeavor doubly painful." She felt that the contemporary notion of femininity embodied the corrupted power relations of civilization, and argued that if women were to advance in society and educational institutions, they had to be seen as intellectually and psychologically equal to men (Todd, 2000). Only later in the 19th century did another work prove as influential, that being John Stuart Mill's *The Subjection of Women* (1869), much of which was based on Wollstonecraft's earlier work (Cunningham, 1978).

In the late 18th century high economic inflation made earning extra income through writing attractive to many women in both America and England. While novels written by women during this period did explore domestic issues, practical concerns, and social intrigues, they also provided a medium through which women could voice positions on women's rights (Lang-Peralta, 1999). Virginia Woolf in *A Room of One's Own* vividly describes the development of women writers in England in the 18th century.

> The extreme activity of mind which showed itself in the later eighteenth centu-
> ry among women—the talking, and the meeting, the writing of essays on
> Shakespeare, the translating of the classics—was founded on the solid fact that
> women could make money by writing. Money dignifies what is frivolous if
> unpaid for. It might still be well to sneer at "bluestockings with an itch for
> scribbling," but it could not be denied that they could put money in their
> purses. Thus, towards the end of the eighteenth century a change came about
> which, if I were rewriting history, I should describe more fully and think of
> greater importance than the Crusades or the Wars of the Roses. The middle-
> class woman began to write. (Woolf, 1929, p. 65)

The so-called "New Woman" writers emerged out of this background in England, and both widespread education and reading played a central role. Many of the New Women were Oxbridge trained and extensive readers, as typically were their heroines. In England, what became known as the new "woman's novels," written largely by and for women, became very popular. These widely distributed works were different than those by male authors in that they were often vocal about sex, venereal disease, contraception, adultery, and divorce as never before.

According to Cunningham (1978), there were two main types of New Woman fiction: the first was the purity school, which focused on the feminine ideal. The typical plotline of these novels was to show the heroine arriving at her ideals of freedom and equality, but then through hard experience becoming disillusioned. The heroine was essentially a man's woman— instinctive, capricious, regularly disturbing the peace of men. The second was the neurotic school in which women were plagued by a variety of neurosis to overcome and suffer through.

Significant social changes occurred in England in the 19th century in both the education of women, and in terms of employment. In the 1890s in England the educational establishment was giving ground as Queen's and Bedford Colleges in London, in 1848 and 1849 respectively, produced qualified women teachers, and a pipeline of students. In 1869 the founding of Girton gave women the first foot in the door of Oxford and Cambridge.

At the same time, women began to be employed in England not only as teachers and nurses, but also in business firms. The growth was rapid as seen by census figures which showed no female clerks in 1861, growing thirty years later to almost 18,000. The modern women's movement in England was largely middle class, coming from these growing occupations, and it was understood that poor women had additional challenges beyond what they had faced (Cunningham, 1978).

This increasing visibility of women in English society led to controversy. An example is shown in an 1868 *Saturday Review* series of articles called "The Girl of the Period" which lamented that the fair young English girl of the past had become little more than a prostitute who dyes her hair, paints her face, talks boldly, likes fashion and money, and is dissatisfied with ordinary life. Uncensored reading by women was often blamed for women's growing frankness in discussing human sexuality. However, by the end of the century, another article in the *Saturday Review* appeared entitled "Dies Dominaie, by a Woman of the Day," a spirited defense of the New Woman which marked the evolution of public opinion.

Major novelists of the time such as Thomas Hardy, George Meredith, and George Gissing also wrote about topics associated with the New Women novelists of the 1890s. Their striking, feminist fiction had heroines who refused to conform to society, and who possessed new ideas about marriage, childbirth, and work. Hardy's three major novels embody ideas of central interest to the New Woman. His Tess character is a powerful indictment of the double moral standard of the time, and Jude was typical of the neurotic New Woman novel school. During this time period at the end of the 19th century, the introduction to England of Zola and French naturalists, along with the Russians, Tolstoy and Dostoevsky, also had a big impact on British writers (Miller, 1997).

Studies of fiction usually focus on the 1890s rather than the years following the turn of the century, and generally assume women ceased to be a dominant force in fiction after the decline of the New Woman novel. Edwardian novels about women and feminism are not often appreciated for their role in developing the modern novel. For instance, George Egerton's (pseudonym of Mary Chavelita Dunne) short story collection *Keynotes* (1893), with her new realism style, influenced D. H. Lawrence and Virginia Woolf. In discussing the future of the novel in 1900, Henry James noted the "revolution taking place in the position and outlook of women." In addition to novels, the fragmentary and inconclusive nature of the short story made it ideal for fictional explorations of the modern woman and feminism (Miller, 1997).

The Edwardian novels were often about the ways in which feminism was changing British society and individual lives. What was initially designated the Marriage Question in the 1880s became in the Edwardian era the Marriage Problem. Women began to marry later, and higher education and employment opportunities led to changes. Legal changes in Britain also pushed change, with married Edwardian women for the first time able to own property and retain custody of children in divorce.

Smaller families became typical in middle- and upper-class families. There was a general feeling that relations between the sexes were breaking down, and this was reflected in novels. A distinctly Edwardian dilemma arose, that of society in transition, and an awareness of the cracks in the old social structures, yet at the same time not having anything clearly new with which to replace them. Then the Suffrage Movement gave feminists a structure for their actions, and provided a new focus for novelists (Miller, 1997).

The period of the New Woman fiction evolves into the pre-WWI period with E.F. Benson, E.V. Lucas, and H.G. Wells, who all take the liberated woman as representative of the age. According to Cunningham (1978), this trend in writing led to the emancipation of the novel form which emerged at the beginning of the 20th century in England. Wells and May Sinclair were two of the best-known novelists of the Edwardian age and both were interested in feminism and a self-conscious modernity.

Wells's *Ann Veronica* (1909) is the best-known and most notorious of Edwardian novels about feminism's impact on the modern woman. The scandalous plot, for that time period, is about a young woman who lives in London on her own and runs off with a married biology professor. It was condemned by critics. However, the sexual frankness and unconventional morality in the popular book was said to represent a transition to the modern novel (Miller, 1997).

In the 1930s, six writers, Dorothy L. Sayers, Muriel Jaeger, Doreen Wallace, Margaret Kennedy, Winifred Holtby, and Vera Brittain, all of whom had attended the groundbreaking women's college at Oxford, became known as the "Somerville School of Novelists." Many other writers of the time made reference to women's higher education, but none in England wrote explicitly about it as did the Somerville novelists. They were popular writers and wrote about their early college experience at Oxford, including descriptions of the early days of college with comparatively bad food, lodging, and plumbing. These writers also described the social context characterized by stiff opposition from many men to their presence at Oxford (Leonardi, 1989).

The Somerville novelists described to the public readership the marginalized position of female students, embodied in how the buildings of Somerville were located at the edge of town, away from the male center. More like American coordinates rather than women's colleges, the Oxford women's colleges were at first merely for boarding, chaperoning, and logistical arrangements for those few female students taking advantage of Oxford lectures and tutorials. Oxford men generally pursued romantic relationships with non-students in town, as the female students were considered too dowdy, prudish, and "serious." Men complained of female frivolity, yet were also said to fear female academic competition in college (Leonardi, 1989).

The six Somerville novelists portrayed the time period in their stories, and were also influential on other women writers. Initially, traditional romantic plots and idealized versions of women's lives were typical of this group of authors. However, eventually the Somerville fictions ended up telling quite a different story, one of female communities and complex relationships. In these novels women characters often do what men feared at the time, which was to take over aggressively, reject men and marriage, and even murder men on occasion (Leonardi, 1989).

## AMERICAN WOMEN WRITERS

In America, there was a similar explosion of women writers in the 19th century. By 1820 there were two possible professions for women beyond the homecrafts and housekeeping: teaching and writing. While teaching would become a common profession for women in the 19th century, authorship could lead to more money. Women writers of this time period generally did not see themselves as artists, but rather as craftswomen and professionals. They also usually lacked the classical education needed for the more ambitious literature of the period. These women writers were outside of the artistic male fraternity, and expected to write specifically for their own sex rather than within the great male literary tradition (Baym, 1978).

Women novelists dominated American reading habits for most of the 19th century. Similar to what was seen in England, "Woman's Fiction" in America is defined as works written by women, addressed to women, and telling of the trials and triumphs of a heroine who, in the face of hardship, finds within herself courage and intelligence to overcome. The genre is said to begin in America with Catharine Sedgwick's *New-England Tale* (1822), and led to a series of popular books such as Susan Warner's *Wide, Wide World* (1850), which remained dominantly popular until after 1870. As a rule, mostly middle-class women had sufficient education to write and read these books, and were motivated by the extra income (Baym, 1978).

Novels by American women written between 1820 and 1870 were by far the most popular fiction of the time, and drew large numbers of female readers. The heroine resembled those in fairy tales, performing dazzling exploits to win out in the end. Once the woman character takes herself seriously, she enters the real world and discovers how deplorably she has been underprepared by education and upbringing to deal with it (Baym, 1978). Alcott's *Little Women* was a seminal and influential book, with the motif about middle-class women's need to earn a living (Sicherman, 2010). It is noteworthy that tomboys as characters first became a major literary type in the 1860s. They were admired up to a point where they were expected to become women.

## COLLEGE FICTION

The college novel is an American fictional genre that includes popular forms, as well as some well-known literary efforts. Novels about college helped form public opinion, while at the same time reflecting the realities of the times as seen by the authors. Often loosely autobiographical in nature, these novels tended to focus on coming-of-age stories and the extracurricular side of college, especially football in male stories.

Kramer's (1981) annotated bibliography of the American college novel lists hundreds published over two centuries, especially numerous at the beginning of the 20th century. The generally recognized first novel set at a college was Nathaniel Hawthorne's *Fanshawe* published in 1828. However, this was a very early effort, one from a literary author that separates it from the majority of the college novel genre. A stereotypical character often found in these early efforts is a student from a poor family—socially challenged by the advantaged culture of college. Generally, this sympathetic character is surrounded by wealthy and silly roommates for contrast, as in the 1886 *Two College Girls* by Helen Dawes Brown.

In the last decades of the 19th century, college novels spoke about early women pioneers in college education, then became novels of celebration of their special campus life, and finally turned to serious examinations of the college experience. Novels of this period present a "green world" of a women's space with its own rules and the opportunity for women to find themselves like nowhere else in society of the time. One consistent concern in these novels is the image of a college-bred woman and evolving standards of womanliness (Marchalonis, 1995).

Published in 1912, *Stover at Yale* is one of the most famous and influential college novels. Dink Stover became the archetype of the college man of the era. Ideas of privilege and open competition are in the forefront of this novel. Predictably, despite Dink's acts of non-conformity, he ultimately wins the highest honor of membership into the famous Skull and Bones club. The novel portrays confusion about the position of college in society, but seems to support the right of individuals to express dissenting opinion and go against the conformist high society as represented by Yale.

The growth of college enrollments after World War I and the increasing public debate over the standards and content of higher education accounts for the great number of college novels published since the 1920s (Lyons, 1962). As early as the 1920s, novels begin to emerge which are more realistic in style and deal with the circumstances of being in college in true-life terms. Credited as one of the first realistic looks at university life, Clarkson Crane's *The Western Shore,* published in 1925, was written in the emerging social realism style of the period and portrayed a group of students attending the University of California at Berkeley. This well-written novel features working-class students, portrayals of clumsy, ambivalent youthful male-female relationships, Jewish and gay students, but no football.

According to Marchalonis (1995), between the 1870s and 1930s a significant subgenre of the college novel emerged portraying the experiences of women going to college. The overall numbers of these books are small, but along with magazine articles and popular press there was much discussion of the college woman and her experiences by 1890. The earliest versions of the fictional portrayals include *An American Girl and Her Four Years in a Boys College* by Olive San Louie Anderson (1878), Helen Dawes Brown's *Two College Girls* (1886), and Abbe Carter Goodloe's *College Girls* (1895). Also, a magazine serial, *A Brave Girl* (1884), and a group of books by Elizabeth W. Champney starting with *Three Vassar Girls* (1882–1892) were very popular.

Fiction about women's colleges include *The Evolution of Evangeline* (1900), a story set at Smith with a plain freshman who with the help of classmates transforms into a beautiful and stylish campus leader (Horowitz, 1984). Generally, coeducation didn't get the same attention as women's colleges in fiction. In novels set at coeducational colleges the main theme is about the comparative status of women, and the plotlines of these novels often contain secret societies and sororities (Marchalonis, 1995).

As described earlier in Chapter 4, women's colleges of the time did include athletic competition, especially basketball (Horowitz, 1984). Although the women's college novels did not have the same preoccupation with athletics, some covered the subject. These include *The Girls of Central High* (1914), describing the coming of sports to girls in a small town, meeting resistance, and then success, as well as the basketball novel, *Jane Allen of the Sub Team* (1917) by Edith Bancroft.

The type of feminism presented in college novels was contextualized within the time period where women's experiences were regarded as personal relationships rather than social structure issues. Baym (1978) argues that the novels show evidence of change in society, rather than championing a need for social activism. The novels were Victorian in their perception of the self as a social product embedded and constrained. They told stories about emergent selves negotiating social possibilities.

Almost nowhere in this fiction are there political activists as heroes. Often heroes are quietly achieving and inwardly focused on self-development. Unlike males, their world is nonviolent, non-controversial, and noncompetitive. Generally, portrayal of intellectual women is missing except in the *Bryn Mawr* short story collection (Marchalonis, 1995).

In the early 20th century, the press reflected the continuing struggle of women to fit in a male-dominated college life. A 1913 *New York Times* article headlined "When the College Girl Comes Home to Stay" and portrayed the difficulty of college students returning home. The press paralleled the frequent depiction in college novels of the difficult reality of women college graduates—the confused expectations of them and their lack of authentic place in American society.

In popular women's magazines from the time, such as *Ladies' Home Journal*, *Women's Home Companion*, and *Good Housekeeping*, young ladies in college were regularly covered, and mostly stressed fun over academics. Women's colleges had generally good press in the early 20th century, and fixated on campus life filled with pranks, trials and joys, athletics and dramatics (Horowitz, 1984).

Turn of the century short story collections such as *Smith College Stories*, *Vassar Stories*, *Wellesley Stories*, and *A Book of Bryn Mawr Stories* were high points in women's fiction writing about colleges, representing women's colleges positively as strong communities of women. College as a place of transformation for young women was a central theme, as well as love of the college and loyalty to it. Instead of the sports which dominate men's college novels, there is typically pursuit of honor societies and triumphs in the dramatic arts (Marchalonis, 1995).

In general, novels set on college campuses became increasingly realistic during and after World War II. James T. Farrell (1943; 1963) wrote two novels that were autobiographical, including one set in Chicago about a commuter student in the late 1920s and another about its central character attending the University of Chicago while working at a gas station. Books about outsiders to the college world were common such as *The Corpus of Joe Bailey (1953),* which tells the story of a poor student from San Diego attending the University of California at Berkeley who never adjusts to middle-

**Figure 5.4.   For the Benefit of the Girl About to Graduate (1890). *Charles Howard Johnson (Library of Congress).***

class life in or after college. Non-traditional students became more commonly understood by the public in the latter half of the 20th century and were portrayed in novels such as *Continuing Education*, (1979), about a 38-year-old woman with three kids who returns to college to study art, and *Night School*, (1961), which profiles an evening education program in New York City.

As women in college became more common by the 1920s the fiction changed to focus on the evils of snobbery and defined social groups. Later college women fiction shows disintegration and a lack of isolated space, with plotlines centered on resistance or adventure. Whereas one characteristic of pre-1930s books is the women with no career ambitions, in the 1950s one finds more career orientation, undoubtedly reflecting the reality of the times. By the 1960s, there were more serious books about women in college, often focused on dysfunctional families and dangers outside the academy (Marchalonis, 1995).

## COLLEGE FILMS

How are women students portrayed in film? College became a regular subject of American films starting early in the silent film era, where, like the college novel, they both formed and reflected the image of higher education of the specific time period. Since the 1920s, these films indicate that the social side of college life was viewed by the public as the most distinctive and interesting aspect of the collegiate experience, the one most worthy of their attention in public entertainments (Berg, 2010).

Wiley Lee Umphlett, in his book *The Movies Go to College (1984)*, argues that college was used as a setting in films because it provided an environment where individuals have the opportunity to revitalize or remake themselves—a characteristically American preoccupation. College films often show the social tension of youthful idealism faced with the reality of the world, which then leads to individual transformation. Characters in college films find their dreams don't match reality. In this way college is portrayed finally as a place for intense socialization.

The overall plotline of college films often involved a transformation of the main character through revising an innocent idealistic self. A good example of this point is the popular *The Freshman*, portrayed by the comedian Harold Lloyd as "Speedy," a young man desperately trying to fit in. Speedy makes one social blunder after another as he attempts to present a successful social image of himself, a particularly American obsession according to some observers (Berg, 2010).

*Naughty but Nice* (1927) is a female version of *The Freshman*, and shows a naïve country girl attending a fancy finishing school that ends with a better understanding of herself. Overall, both films reveal an anti-intellectual message of the individual versus the dominant system. In the early forties, campuses also became a favorite setting for MGM musicals such as *Girl Crazy* (1943) and *Bathing Beauty* (1944).

After World War II, college films shifted their focus to depict college as the ticket to success in life; this shift, of course, coincided with the G.I. Bill and influx of middle and lower-class students into post-secondary education. However, women didn't fare as equitably; in the '50s and '60s the myth of women going to college only to get married was perpetuated in various Hollywood romantic comedies.

This decade and a half of images presenting the American Dream in college was followed closely by a more realistic portrayal in the '60s, '70s, and '80s. *The Young Lovers* released in 1964 is one of the first films to offer a truthful depiction of college life. Perhaps as college became more common place it lost some of its mythical power in the collective American imagination. Films such as *The Graduate* (1967) and *Carnal Knowledge* (1971) are prime examples of the changed public image of college presented in the '60s and '70s. On the other hand, the 1970 box office hit *Love Story*, based on the best-selling novel by Erich Segal, about the heir of an American upper-class East Coast family attending Harvard College where he meets a working-class Radcliffe College student, deliberately steered clear of the social change occurring at the time.

Reflecting the historical era evolving out of the Vietnam War, some movies epitomize the rebellion of middle- and upper-class students against the role college seemed to play as an instrument of conformity and path to affluence. *Educating Rita* was one of the first films to tell the story of non-traditional students in a story about a British student at the Open University who tries to make good through education. Mary McCarthy's well-known bestselling novel and later film, *The Group* (1963), depicts her experience at Vassar.

In the last 40 years representations of college in American film have become more critical and realistic. More recent films about women in college with themes of empowerment include *Legally Blond* (2001), *Mona Lisa Smile* (2003), and *Pitch Perfect* (2012). Women athletes also became a popular topic with films such as *A League of Their Own* (1992), *Bend it Like Beckham* (2002), *Million Dollar Baby* (2004), and *Battle of the Sexes* (2017).

Generally, college is often seen in contemporary film as a place where studying isn't very important and personal issues are paramount. The depictions of college professors are usually negative, and higher education ill prepares students for the challenges of the real world (Berg, 2010).

## CONCLUSION

In this chapter the experiences of women learning informally through reading and continuing education was examined. In response to exclusion from advanced education, women pursued intellectual development and creative expression through reading, writing, and meeting in their homes to discuss books and ideas. One of the reasons women were able to succeed academically so quickly when finally allowed into college was because they had invested their energy into reading and writing. This practice served women well in the text-heavy curriculum of college.

The fact that reading was allowed, or tolerated, gave women a private space to develop their minds, and better understand a world that was often not available to them experientially. In addition to the private learning, women early on read and discussed books in groups in their homes. This practice led easily into forms of continuing education epitomized by, first, the highly influential Chautauqua Movement, and then later the New School in New York City. Continuing education was the initial way for women to attend lectures as auditors at Harvard, becoming more formally the Annex, until Radcliffe College was formed as a separate coordinate college. Women students were also heavily involved in forms of distance learning beginning in the 19th century, undoubtedly because of the accessibility, and this trend continues today.

Writing for women was a natural development because it was something that could be done in private in the home. Additionally, because the writing was sometimes directed at other women rather than men, it wasn't seen as socially threatening. Nevertheless, an inherent tension existed from the start between the freedom of women writing, and the rigid structure within which they had to operate. Virginia Woolf summarized the inherent contradiction of women writing when she describes the women's writers in 19th-century England:

> One has only to skim those old forgotten novels and listen to the tone of voice in which they are written to divine that the writer was meeting criticism; she was saying this by way of aggression, or that by way of conciliation. She was admitting that she was "only a woman," or protesting that she was "as good as a man." She met that criticism as her temperament dictated, with docility and diffidence, or with anger and emphasis. It does not matter which it was; she was thinking of something other than the thing itself. Down comes her book upon our heads. There was a flaw in the centre of it. And I thought of all the women's novels that lie scattered, like small pock-marked apples in an orchard, about the second-hand book shops of London. It was the flaw in the centre that had rotted them. She had altered her values in deference to the opinion of others. (Woolf, 1929, p. 74)

Nevertheless, women writers gained an occupation, and importantly prepared themselves for higher education.

The specific genres of college fiction and film reveal the experience of women as they began to enter college in America, and emphasize the struggle of female students to find themselves and their place in a male-dominated society. By focusing in some cases on low-income students at coeducational colleges, and then women from affluent families in women's colleges, the genre as a whole reveals the complexity of the college-going experience.

The next chapter takes up the development starting in the late 1960s of Women's Studies programs and feminist pedagogical approaches. Women of this time period began to ponder the differences from men in what women want to study (curricula), and how they learn (pedagogy).

## DISCUSSION QUESTIONS

1. Describe the important ways that various forms of informal learning have impacted women leading up to participation in college.
2. How did salons, reading circles, and book clubs develop?
3. How did women writers become an important source and influence on the education of women?
4. Describe the characteristics of fiction and film representations of women in college.
5. What was the importance of continuing education in the education of women?

*Chapter Six*

# Late 20th-Century Scholarly and Pedagogical Approaches

The first American increase of women in college that occurred between 1910 and 1930 coincided with the Suffrage Movement. The social activism of women was both a cause and effect of the newly opened doors to college. Historically linked to the abolitionists prior to the Civil War and the Settlement House Movement, the suffragettes often found supporters in female college students. Women college graduates became increasingly fervent voices in the national debate about voting, property, and divorce rights.

The second historical boom of women students enrolled in American universities at the end of the 20th century coincided with the wide-ranging social change occurring in the 1960s. The anti-Vietnam War protest, and especially the Civil Rights movement, helped to power feminism, and subsequently changes in the university. From the early days of the feminist movement, two main areas were targeted for change in the academy: what is taught and how it is taught.

The pressure to add Black Studies programs in colleges was followed by pushes for Women's Studies curricular supplements. Additionally, faculty members began to talk and write about alternative teaching methods that might appeal to young women students. This chapter contemplates the unique efforts made for women students that arose out of this period of great social change: Women's Studies and feminist pedagogy.

## WOMEN'S STUDIES

Women's Studies as an academic discipline first appeared in the latter half of the 1960s when faculty began to create new courses that facilitated reflection

**Figure 6.1.   Harriet Tubman, full-length portrait, seated in chair, facing front, probably at her home in Auburn, New York (1911).** *Unknown photographer (Library of Congress Rare Book and Special Collections Division).*

on the female experience and feminist aspirations. Their efforts at course development were inspired by both the Civil Rights Movement, and the model of Black Studies (Boxer, 1988). Courses and programs on women began to appear at a number of universities, such as at Cornell University where Sheila Tobias called for a new discipline of "Female Studies" (Boxer, 1988). That specific program led Tobias to the creation of an influential series of ten books first published in 1970, in which practitioners of Female or Women's Studies shared their syllabi, reading lists, and teaching experiences (Boxer, 1988).

Between 1970 and 1975, 150 new Women's Studies programs were founded, and 150 more between 1975 and 1980. During this time the number of individual courses also grew to an estimated 30,000 nationwide. By 1984, Women's Studies programs were offered at 195 universities at the BA level, 50 at the master's, and 18 at the doctoral (Boxer, 1988).

The National Women's Studies Association (NWSA) was created in 1977 and defined its discipline in activist terms as "educational strategy" for change (Bowles & Klein, 1983). The central conflict for many since the beginning of Women's Studies was whether or not to integrate and incorporate new feminist perspectives into the current majors, or to create a separate discipline. Some argued that to bring women fully into the curriculum meant to reorganize all previously constructed knowledge, and to change what and how it is taught.

Furthermore, from the start Women's Studies programs were seen as not just academic programs, but places to encourage political activism. Specifically, the leaders saw the need to challenge economic, political, cultural, and psychological imperatives based on gender (Culley & Portuges, 1985). Adrienne Rich suggested what needed to be asked was what women should know:

> Does she not, as a self-conscious, self-defining human being, need a knowledge of her own history, her much politicized biology, an awareness of the creative work of women of the past, the skills and crafts and techniques and powers exercised by women in different times and cultures, a knowledge of women's rebellions and organized movements against our oppression and how they have been routed or diminished. . . . I would suggest that not biology, but ignorance of ourselves, has been the key to our powerlessness. (Rich, 1985, p. 24)

It was argued at the start that the challenge for Women's Studies was for scholars to essentially rewrite each discipline's history, critique its canon, and question the basic assumptions, beliefs, and objectives of their fields. Done effectively, it was said, feminist scholars changed the way a subject was studied and written about (MacNabb, Cherr, Popham & Prys, 2001).

For example, English composition needed to be expanded to allow different ways of writing that include the personal (which was sometimes identified as more naturally female). Similarly, objective truth in scientific and sociological fields came under question, changing the way so-called "facts" were interpreted. In philosophy, feminists claimed that alternative, nonargumentative forms of discussion and analysis might be used, incorporating subjective experiences. Overall, feminist scholarship was concerned with representations of women and sought to force the disciplines to look beyond their own fields and consider the larger context (MacNabb, Cherr, Popham, & Prys, 2001).

The criticism of the positivist objectivity in the field of social sciences has been a particular focus in Women's Studies. Scholars in this new discipline argued that human behavior is complex and difficult to put into neat categories. Alternatively, research in the social sciences should be conscious of collective bias, as well as the point of view of the individual researcher (Bowles & Klein, 1983).

Some have expressed concerns about the organizational position of the Women's Studies programs in the university. In the beginning it was typical for these degree programs to be handled in a cross-disciplinary fashion with an assigned coordinating faculty member working with faculty in other departments in a committee fashion. Often a few tenured faculty members taught core courses, with lecturers from across disciplines filling in to teach the rest (Boxer, 1989).

Critics complained that the programs too often were isolated and powerless, leading to the "ghettoization" of women who taught in those majors. Others argued that such a structural position was a refuge, not a ghetto. Still more raised the larger question of whether or not feminism had in retrospect significantly transformed the mainstream college curriculum (Quinn, 2003).

Nevertheless, many consistently argued for a separate program: "We believe that autonomous Women's Studies programs, in constant interaction with the community, hold the potential for contributing to changes in the present power relationships in society at large" (Bowles & Klein, 1983, p. 13). The tension between academics and activists in Women's Studies persisted until the 1980s when seeing value in both approaches became the typical thinking on the debate over separate Women's Studies programs (Boxer, 1988).

Bowles and Klein (1983) suggest that strategies for successful Women Studies programs include a commitment from the top, the personal recruitment of students and faculty, mentoring, network formation for students, and a solid feedback system. Pearson, Shavlik and Touchton (1989) claim that a concentration on education for and about men has led to the current shape of the traditional higher education curriculum, and that questions of gender sameness and difference are complex. In some ways men's and women's educational needs are similar. At the same time, women by themselves share common experiences, societal definitions, and treatment. But women also differ in background attitudes, experience, age, race, ethnic groups, and sexual preference. They also vary in learning and leadership styles. None of these unique qualities or differences should be ignored by educators (Pearson, Shavlik & Touchton, 1989).

# FEMINIST PEDAGOGY

Ropers-Huilman and Palmer (2008) define feminist educational methods as valuing experiences as sources of interdisciplinary knowledge, recognizing gender effects on the learning process and power hierarchies between teachers and learners, and finally it draws attention to the role of education in social change. One of the primary principals of feminist pedagogy is that it legitimizes personal references in intellectual inquiry, something that goes against male traditions which typically value scientific "objectivity." This new feminist pedagogy understands from the start that knowledge is not neutral (Culley & Portuges, 1985).

Adrienne Rich wrote that "it is not easy to think like a woman in a man's world, in the world of the professions; yet the capacity to do that is a strength which we can try to help our students develop. To think like a woman in a man's world means thinking critically, refusing to accept the givens, making connections between facts and ideas which men have left unconnected" (Rich, 1985, p. 28).

Similarly, Carol Gilligan, in her highly influential book *In a Different Voice* (1993), argued that women suffer from trying to fit into existing male models of human development which omit a woman's voice: "What emerges in these voices is a sense of vulnerability that impedes these women from taking a stand, what George Eliot regards as the girl's 'susceptibility' to adverse judgments by others, which stems from her lack of power and consequent inability 'to do something in the world'" (Gilligan, p. 66).

Paulo Freire, the well-known educational scholar-philosopher in his book *Pedagogy of the Oppressed* (1970), was fundamental to feminist pedagogy early on because, although he did not specifically discuss women as an oppressed group, he gave a framework for understanding disadvantage in education. Freire's theory of the pedagogy of liberation for oppressed groups was attractive to women thinking about educational approaches for women (Quinn, 2003). Freire's notion of the teacher as joint learner made sense to feminists, although some claim he failed to address the various forms of power held by teachers depending on race, gender, and settings. Furthermore, Freire supported the concept of positivist universal truth, which generally goes against fundamental feminist theory centered on personal knowledge (Holland, Blair, & Sheldon, 1995).

Two important debates that arose from feminist pedagogy are in regard to the hard sciences, and secondly with qualitative versus quantitative research methods in the social sciences. Historically, some scholars argued that the sciences were appropriated during the 17th century as a masculine domain, and that they were intimately embroiled with the structures of power in industrial society. On the other hand, some women scientists perceived the feminist critique as putting forth an unsophisticated characterization of science that reinforces traditional stereotypes, and works against positive social change (Longino & Hammonds, 1995).

The feminist critique of science tracked those of the counter-culture movement of the 1960s, but was more threatening in some ways because of questioning the division of labor and identity. As one scholar remarked, "Women have been more systematically excluded from doing serious science than from performing any other social activity except, perhaps, frontline warfare" (Harding, 1986, p. 31). Harding (1986) claims that the social division of labor by gender, and the construction of individual gender identity, have structurally affected the history of science. By questioning traditional science, feminist thinkers have challenged the intellectual and social orders at their very foundations.

> Science functions primarily as a "black box": whatever the moral and political values and interests responsible for selecting problems, theories, methods, and interpretations of research, they reappear at the other end of the inquiry as the moral and political universe that science projects as natural and thereby helps to legitimate. (Harding, 1986, pp. 250–251)

Feminists often advocate qualitative research methods to capture individual women's understandings, emotions, and actions on their own terms. However, quantitative method defenders worry that qualitative approaches have few safeguards against research biases, and abandon traditional methodology which disadvantages them with peers in the academy (Holland, Blair & Sheldon, 1995).

Some contend that feminist pedagogy has been easier to implement than Women's Studies. Others argue that feminist pedagogy is a fragmented concept and practice. While it is logical to use pedagogy to give women voice in the classroom, Quinn (2003) notes that "The mass entry of women students is the most dramatic change universities have ever seen. Yet if institutions are indeed being transformed, it is not necessarily by or for women. Although HE can be perceived as a protected space, it cannot be seen as a feminist one, in terms of what is learned and how it is studied" (p. 148).

## CONCLUSION

Women's Studies and feminist pedagogy need to be appreciated in the context within which they arose in the 1970s. As Carol Gilligan wrote, "When women feel excluded from direct participation in society, they see themselves as subject to a consensus of judgment made and enforced by the men on whose protection and support they depend and by whose names they are known" (Gilligan, 1993, p. 67). One reason for the policy and administrative conflicts seen at colleges between men and women in the late 20th century is a result of the rapid transition from one social system of gender roles to another, and they indicate a struggle for progress toward more egalitarian roles.

By the 1970s and 80s, scholars pointed to inconsistent mutual expectations of men and women. On the psycho-social level Komarovsky (1985) noted that men should not be socialized to suppress emotions, and women should not be socialized to feel that self-confidence and ambition to succeed are abrasive. Some point out that research about sex differences frequently contain gross procedural errors. For years scientists concluded that boys were better at math than girls, overlooking the fact that the reason may be that boys take more math classes (Fausto-Sterling, 1992).

One very important change in the United States coming out of the feminist movement was the increased use of birth control (especially the pill), and then the legalization of abortion in the 1973 landmark decision of *Roe v. Wade*. Gilligan notes the psychological importance of the idea of free choice prompted by the new legal interpretation: "When birth control and abortion provide women with effective means for controlling their fertility, the dilemma of choice enters a central arena of women's lives" (Gilligan, 1993, p. 70).

While some female faculty and administrators I questioned were very supportive of women's and gender studies programs, others were skeptical about the future importance and impact of such disciplines: "I don't see that happening as few actually take these courses/programs and those who do, have an activist leaning already." Some female respondents expressed a negative response to Women's Studies programs. "While the stated goal is equality, I see a divisive side to such programs in the form of male resistance driven in part by the failure to reach out to male students. There is little to no effort to incorporate any understanding of male ideology, and not as a biological necessity (it's not) within a society that requires men to repress anything passive and feminine and the cost of giving this up. The reality of gender differences is exaggerated in these programs. These programs are driven by ideology not science—a fact that weakens the entire field."

In terms of classroom experiences, some respondents felt it was logical to assume some differences in the way men and women teach: "I think there is no doubt that an academic's point of view is influenced by his/her gender, and it seems logical that many of these professors would draw upon 'feminist teaching approaches,' along with other pedagogical strategies." Yet others did not see an important influence in feminist approaches: "My experience in the classroom was that faculty were intentionally more feminist and inclusive, while female students rejected feminism and largely misunderstood it."

Overall, those surveyed for this book generally expressed a lessening role in the future for Women's Studies programs, perhaps as an evolution of the field. "I think these programs remain relatively small and I think if you want to study these you will regardless," and "That feels a bit ghettoized to me, at this point." Finally, some did express concern about the practical wisdom of majoring in these fields: "I do wonder if majoring in fields such as these will provide enough women with job opportunities after graduation."

In the next chapter the book ends by analyzing the patterns and themes unearthed throughout the examination of the statistics on women in higher education, historical background in women's and coeducational colleges, college athletics and public policy, informal ways of learning and intellectual development, and the perspectives presented in this chapter on Women's Studies and feminist pedagogy.

## DISCUSSION QUESTIONS

1. In what ways are Women's Studies programs still relevant today?
2. How do current female undergraduates perceive Women's Studies and Feminist Pedagogy?
3. In what ways do men and women learn differently?
4. Are qualitative versus quantitative research methods gendered?
5. In what ways are hard sciences legitimately challenged by feminist arguments of bias?

# Conclusion

## *What Does the Future Hold?*

I've learned a great deal in writing this book. Probably more than in any other research I've done over the years, this project has surprised and sparked insights. Although previous investigation touched on some aspects of women in college, I lacked a full grasp of the intricacies of this history. I conclude in this chapter with an appreciation of the complexity of the social history of gender and education, and a belief that understanding the particulars is essential in moving forward effectively toward meaningful global equality.

The book started in the first chapter by looking at the background and context of women in higher education, as well as presenting statistics on change in female student involvement, and faculty and university administration composition. The history of the resistance to women entering the academy was described, with a look at the various institutional types that arose in the late 19th century, including men-only, women-only, coordinate, and co-educational colleges. The specific pattern of the increase of both female faculty members and university administrators was evaluated, especially for faculty in attaining equal raw numbers, and more modest increases in the leadership ranks.

However, on closer examination in this chapter, we observed the lack of parity between men and women in compensation, rank, academic discipline, and institutional type. The general inference reached was that the positive news of increased participation is tempered by the appreciation that inequalities remain in compensation and less employment in more prestigious disciplines and elite institutions. Finally, the important issue of student debt was discussed, showing greater average debt for female students subsequent to graduation, partly a result of earning on average 80% of that earned by males.

In Chapter 2, the larger global background of the tertiary education of women was considered, along with literacy and economic development matters. While by the year 2000 women worldwide equaled men in higher education, large disparities persist in the important STEM majors. The association between reduced childbirth rates and increased higher education was explored, as well as the changing legal and political environments addressing reproductive and property rights for women around the globe. Additionally, in this chapter figures on comparative gender skills worldwide and their possible causes were scrutinized, revealing that assumptions about innate differences are often overvalued. Finally, the increasing leadership roles for women in public office, and the connection between the education of women and economic development was described.

In Chapter 3, the controversial development of women's, coordinate, and coeducational colleges in the 19th and early 20th centuries was outlined. The history of the women's college movement developing in response to exclusion from men-only institutions was traced, along with the unique differences in aims and specific curricula of these schools. The rapid growth of coeducational institutions following the Civil War was funded largely by the Morrill Act of 1862 and spurred on by growing women's social activism, a need for classroom teachers, and a literate population with more leisure time as a result of industrialization.

Then specific colleges were profiled in order to get a sense of the uniqueness of institutions serving female students across America, including the Catholic HBCU Xavier University of Louisiana, the New School comprised predominantly of women and emphasizing continuing education, Catholic Mount Saint Mary's University serving low-income and minority women, and Scripps College, a West Coast Ivy-women's college.

Chapter 4 presented the landmark Title IX legislation in America, and followed the positive impact on both women's sports and university climate. The complex historical setting was presented, as well as data revealing the massive impact of Title IX legislation on the growth of collegiate women's athletics. The divergent history of women's athletics was investigated, which was more closely tied to academic departments than men's, and has led to women in sports academically outperforming males. The chapter finished with a discussion of critical perspectives, and the media representation of the significant social change that the visibility of women athletes has caused.

Chapter 5 analyzed how women in America and Europe gained literacy through informal ways of learning that prepared them for successful entrance into the academy. The importance of alternative ways of learning, and expressing themselves through writing and reading in the late 18th and 19th centuries was explored. In particular, the 19th-century women's novels that dominated England and America, as well as aspects of informal learning practices such as salons, reading circles, and continuing education groups like the Chautauqua Movement, were investigated in this chapter. College fiction and film in America were analyzed to better appreciate the emerging vehicles for women writers, and the depiction of women in popular media. This chapter presented an aspect of women in higher education that helps to explain why women were so successful in college once restrictions were slowly lifted—advantages in literacy that continue today.

**Figure C.1. Looking Backward (1912).** *From* Life, *August 22, 1912, p. 1638 (Library of Congress).*

Chapter 6 considered late 20th-century approaches to the advanced education of women that came about in conjunction with the Civil Rights and Feminist Movements of the 1960s and 1970s. By the 1980s, Women's Studies programs became common in American universities beset with ongoing internal debates about the wisdom of creating bifurcated academic departments as opposed to incorporating new viewpoints within existing curricula. Feminist pedagogy arose at the same time with the idea that women's ways of knowing and learning had not been previously honored in the traditional university. The chapter considered contemporary viewpoints on both how Women's or Gender Studies, and feminist pedagogy are viewed in the academy today.

## THEMES

In looking back over this very complex subject a number of important themes emerge. While one could point to others, the following stand out to the author.

• The gender gap favors women in education, but men in the labor market.

While it is a cause for celebration that women now equal men in participation in advanced higher education, worldwide women still have an annual income of roughly 80% of that of men. Figure C.2 displays the pattern over time in America. While the average income gap has narrowed, in 2017 women still made 80.5% of what men did.

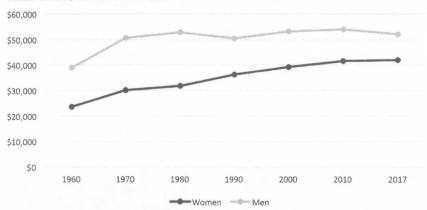

**Figure C.2. Average Full-Time Wage Comparison by Gender. *U.S. Census, 2018.***

Multiple reasons for this discrepancy are given by various experts in the field, including breaks in careers because of childbirth and rearing, and women in lower paying types of employment. Nevertheless, it is hard to get past the raw compensation gap between men and women.

Clearly, the problem of gendered college majors, discussed in Chapter 2, creates separate pathways to employment in different sectors for men and women. Additionally, in higher education itself we saw in Chapter 1 the same 80% of men's compensation for female faculty members. The lower compensation and placement in presidential positions of women is one more important variance in the labor market.

Gains have also been made specifically in the employment of college-educated women in the workforce. According to a new Pew Research Center analysis of data from the U.S. Bureau of Labor Statistics, women are approaching a milestone in gender parity with 2019 likely to be the first year in which they are a majority of the college-educated labor force. This trend is important because of the strong correlation between college education and income (Pew Research Center, 2019).

One significant factor in the slowness of college-educated women to equal men in the workforce is that they are less likely than their male counterparts to enter the labor force after graduation. In 2018, 69.9% of college-educated women were in the labor force, compared with 78.1% of college-educated men. The number of women with at least a bachelor's degree would have had to significantly outstrip the number of college-educated men to offset this labor force involvement difference (Pew Research Center, 2019).

Though women are at parity with men in the overall college-educated labor force, they lag significantly behind in many specific occupations, with only 25% in computer occupations and 15% of college-educated workers in engineering occupations. In sum, we have positive news in women increasingly going to and succeeding in college, and entering the workforce, tempered by consistent and persistent inequality in high-paying occupations and wages (Pew Research Center, 2019).

- Financial Aid debt threatens to reverse gains by women in higher education.

The fact that women on average leave college with greater debt is indeed troubling (Chapter 1). Coupled with the previously noted finding regarding lower average income, it is no wonder that women tend to express more concern than males about their finances following graduation from college.

The long-term impact of this pattern of higher debt and lower subsequent income is likely to be reduced participation in college. Or, looked at more constructively, women students may enter college with a more critical eye toward potential careers, and increasingly choose to pursue previously male-dominated STEM occupations. Either way, changes need to be made.

• Childbirth is a central factor in women's education.

Historically, countries around the world experienced increased education of women as birthrates declined. This pattern is linked closely to industrialization, the development of a middle class, and the availability of and attitudes toward birth control. It is difficult to overstate the impact of the change in birthrate on education in America where it drastically declined in the 19th century, directly spurring the attendance of women in college. With the expansion of female education came an extraordinary decline in fertility from an average of seven children in 1810 to three and a half per woman in 1900 (Sicherman, 2010).

The important social changes of women's voting rights, the feminist movement, shifting views of the role of women in society, the division of labor, and more effective birth control methods are connected together with the advanced education of women. Furthermore, for those women in college, childcare concerns continue to have an impact on both female students and faculty members. According one a report, 4.8 million American college students or 26% of all registered students, were raising children. Additionally, a full half, over two million, were single mothers (Lumina Foundation, 2014).

• Internationally, higher education for women has central economic development importance.

Women and poverty internationally are strongly associated. The miserable fact is that most of those who live in a state of poverty are women and children. Childbirth rates and a lack of access to birth control are key factors in women's poverty. The cyclical pattern of childbirth and poverty is a chronic issue for developing countries.

Advanced tertiary education for women can provide a large increase in a nation's workforce, and raise the economic tide for all.

• Women's athletics has helped to positively change college culture.

The large increase in the number of women's teams, and women in college sports since the enactment of Title IX in 1972 tell only part of the success story of this important social legislation in America. The shift in focus for colleges from primarily men's to also encompass women's sports has expanded the overall campus environment. What was a "chilly climate" for women on previously male-preoccupied campuses has changed as women more actively participate in student activities, leadership, and serve as visible role models.

Furthermore, women's athletics offers a more balanced approach to college sports with a focus on human development, rather than a subsequent professional career, and is an exemplary model for all going forward. The fact that women's athletics developed with a strong link to academic programs, unlike men's, cannot be ignored when analyzing the data showing women academically outperforming male athletes. If universities are serious about reforming college athletics, they should start by looking at their own women's programs.

- The tenure system may be contributing to the slow progress toward equity in female faculty rank and compensation.

The positive fact is that women faculty are now approximately equally represented broadly in higher education. The negative reality is that women faculty tend to be disproportionately located in two-year community colleges and the less prestigious four-year institutions. The top-tier research institutions especially continue to look very male in their faculties. Furthermore, across institutional types, women are disproportionately located in lower ranks.

The dominant faculty search, promotion, and tenure system in American higher education, while certainly providing a formal quality control function, may be slowing progress for women faculty. For instance, in one study looking at gender and racial prejudices in faculty hiring in STEM fields (Eaton, Saunders, & Jacobson, 2019), the candidate's name on the curriculum vitae (CV) was used to manipulate race and gender and showed that faculty exhibited a gender bias favoring the male candidates as more competent and more hirable than the otherwise identical female candidates.

In addition to the typical prejudices that some faculty may have toward women in their disciplines, they may enforce more rigid standards in reviewing the academic work of female scholars. During the tenure and promotion review, some male faculty members may be less sympathetic toward family responsibilities that disproportionately burden women faculty.

- Appreciate the complexity of female identities.

One important perspective in looking at various social groups in education is to understand that every individual has a complex identity. Rather than thinking about women as one group, it is important to appreciate the intersection of race, socio-economic status, and age. "Intersectionality" or "intersectional feminism" is a branch of feminism which appreciates how different aspects of social and political discrimination overlap with gender.

Women are at the intersection of many identities that may have different relationships to power, and all women cannot simply be gathered under one label. As Virginia Woolf perceptively wrote: "It would be a thousand pities if women wrote like men, or lived like men, or looked like men, for if two sexes are quite inadequate, considering the vastness and variety of the world, how should we manage with one only?" (Woolf, 1929, p. 88). Overlapping social-group identities shape the experiences of anyone who identifies as a woman.

• Learn from women's colleges best practices.

While there are fewer and fewer women-only colleges, in retrospect there are still important things that can be learned from these institutions and put to use today. Tidball, Smith, Tidball and Wolf-Wendel (1999) point to benefits such as the importance of providing role models in female faculty and administration, establishing a networking function that gives students lifelong contacts, encouraging a generosity of women toward each other, and giving an opportunity for women to study in all fields.

• Learning outside the classroom will continue to be important for women.

Faced with a society that limited women's opportunities for advanced education, other avenues developed outside of formal education, including reading, writing, informal salons and reading groups, and continuing education. While women generally do not have the same formal restrictions on participation in higher education that they once had, there are still unequal levels of family responsibilities. As a result, it is likely that informal learning will continue to be important for women whether it is through simply reading, continuing education, or forms of distance learning.

• Self-confidence is of central importance for female students.

Self-assurance in higher education is especially important for many women. As George Eliot wrote in Middlemarch, "Will not a tiny speck very close to your vision blot out the glory of the world, and leave only a margin by which we see the blot? I know no speck so troublesome as self" (Eliot, 1956, p. 307). Sax (2008) argues that women's strong academic orientation is tempered by a comparatively low academic self-concept. Women outstudy and outperform men in academic achievement, but rate themselves lower on every academic or intellectual scale, with just over half of women considering themselves above average, compared to two-thirds of the men. The gender gap in intellectual self-confidence widens over four years of college, and while women express greater confidence than men in writing, the gap disappears during the four years.

The context in which individuals develop self-confidence is complex, involving family relationships, gender norms and expectations, and personal experience and tendencies. The important lesson here for educational institutions is to pay close attention to this aspect of human development and learning, avoid practices which may harm confidence, and encourage those who may falter in this area.

## FINAL THOUGHTS

Female faculty members and administrators reflected on the overall change in higher education in carefully chosen words: "It has changed the dynamics of the institution and ways in which communication occurs, what services are offered, and I'm sure altered certain behaviors." One emphasized that when looking at the encouraging statistics about women in college it is important not to adopt an attitude of "all is fixed." Furthermore, she pointed out that it will take all in higher education to continue the changes: "It will take both strong female voices and male allies."

In terms of the leadership of universities, the increase of visible female role models was pointed to by colleagues, as well as generally more inclusive management styles. There is "more participatory and collective decision making; increased positive role models for women and the normalizing of women in various positions in the educational landscape." Nevertheless, challenges remain with women respondents speaking about the ongoing challenges to both administrators and faculty to overcome gendered expectations: "Women are expected to be more nurturing and are perceived harshly when they are not ladylike. Hence, women are expected to manage emotion and feelings more than males."

The vital issue of childcare responsibilities for female faculty and administrators arose in the responses: "Persistence of performance expectations are harder to meet for primary caregivers, who are still more likely to be women." Another respondent said, "In combination with the increase in non-traditional age students, there is a need for greater flexibility to accommodate working, parenting, and caring for aging parents." Contrary to the image of increasingly shared home responsibilities, women spoke about the higher burden for women: "In my experience so far, I see a lot of females on whom caretaker burdens fall—for parents or siblings, and sometimes their own children."

Interestingly, some women queried noted the future challenge of explaining and adapting to a female-dominant student population: "I actually see the challenge as explaining/defending/thinking about why there aren't more male students," and "Higher education needs to reconsider how not to unintentionally exclude men while responding to growing numbers of women." Another woman commented, "This sounds crazy, but I have recently wondered about the implications of having so few males. . . . It seems to me that imbalance in either direction isn't good, so while I am very happy to see more women, the huge imbalance is a little worrying. Which takes me back to the puzzle in the first question—where are the men going?" Finally, one administrator summarized her point of view: "I don't think women want to be treated differently—just fairly. Institutions have an opportunity to invest in women students, faculty and administrators and harness their collective potential."

I end this book with an image (Figure C.3) I discovered at the Library of Congress of Vinnie Ream, a young sculptress. Just 18 years old in 1866 when President Lincoln agreed to model for her, she was the youngest and first woman to receive a commission as an artist from the United States government. I am struck by her direct gaze, confidence, and talent.

Education is emancipation.

## DISCUSSION QUESTIONS

1. If a university were to concentrate on meeting the needs of women, what would it do differently?
2. What are the most important lessons learned from the history of women's advanced education?
3. Respond to the themes listed in this chapter.
4. What surprised you to learn in reading this book?
5. Reflect on the personal experiences of women in college (yourself or someone you know).

**Figure C.3. Vinnie Ream at work upon her Lincoln bust which rests upon the stand she used in the White House while President Lincoln posed for her (1865–70).** *Unknown photographer (Library of Congress).*

# References

American Association of University Women (AAUW). (2019). Deeper in debt: Women and student loans. Washington D.C. AAUW. Retrieved from https://www.aauw.org/research/deeper-in-debt/

Acosta/Carpenter. (2015). *Women in intercollegiate sport. A longitudinal, national study, thirty-seven year update. 1977–2014.* Unpublished manuscript. Retrieved from https//www.acostacarpenter.ORG

Adams, E. K. (1923). College students and their communities. *Alumnae Quarterly.* April. South Hadley, MA: Mount Holyoke College.

Adler, J. A. (1994). *Women's colleges.* New York: Prentice Hall.

Aisenberg, N., & Harrington, M. (1988). *Women of academe.* Amherst: The University of Massachusetts Press.

Alam, M.-U., Luby, S. P., Halder, A. K., Islam, K., Opel, A., Shoab, A. K., Ghosh, P. K., Rahman, M., Mahon, T., & Unicomb, L. (2017). Menstrual hygiene management among Bangladeshi adolescent schoolgirls and risk factors affecting school absence: results from a cross-sectional survey. *BMJ Open,* Vol. 7, No. 7, e015508.

Albelda, R., & Tilly, C. (1997). *Glass ceilings and bottomless pits: Women's work, women's poverty.* Boston: South End Press.

Alexander, K. T., Mwaki, A., Adhiambo, D., Cheney-Coker, M., Muga, R., & Freeman, M. C. (2016). The life-cycle costs of school water, sanitation and hygiene access in Kenyan primary schools. *International Journal of Environmental Research and Public Health,* Vol. 13, No. 7, p. 637.

American Association of University Professors (AAUP). (2019). Annual report on economic status of the profession, 2018–19. Retrieved from https://www.aaup.org/2018–19–faculty-compensation-survey-results

American Council on Education. (2017). The American college president study 2017 (ACPS).

American Economic Association. March 18, 2019. AEA professional climate survey: Main findings. Retrieved from https://www.aeaweb.org/resources/member-docs/climate-survey-results-mar-18–2019

Astin, H. S., & Leland, C. (1991). *Women of influence, women of vision: a cross-generational study of leaders and social change.* San Francisco: Jossey-Bass.

Bancroft, E. (1917). *Jane Allen of the Sub Team.* New York: Saalfield Publishing.

Bank, B. J. (2003). *Contradictions in women's education: Traditionalism, careerism, and community at a single-sex college.* New York: Teachers College Press.

Bank, B. J. (ed.) (2007). *Gender and education: An encyclopedia.* Westport, CT: Praeger.

Baym, N. (1978). *Women's fiction: A guide to novels by and about women in America, 1820–1870.* Ithaca, NY: Cornell University Press.

Belanger, K. (2016). *Invisible seasons: Title IX and the fight for equity in college sports.* Syracuse, NY: Syracuse University Press.

Berg, G. A. (2010). *Low-income students and the perpetuation of inequality: Higher education in America.* Surrey, UK: Ashgate Publishing Group.

Boas, L. S. (1935). *Woman's education begins: The rise of the women's colleges.* Norton, MA: Wheaton College Press.

Bollmann, S. (2018). *Women who write are dangerous.* New York: Abbeville Press Publishers.

Bowles, G. & Klein, R. D. (1983). *Theories of women's studies.* London, UK: Routledge & Kegan Paul.

Boxer, M. J. (1988). For and about women: The theory and practice of women's studies in the United States. In Minnich, E., O'Barr, J., & Rosenfeld, R. (eds), *Reconstructing the academy: Women's education and women's studies.* Chicago: University of Chicago Press.

Boxer, J. J. (1989). Women's studies, feminist goals, and the science of women. In Pearson, C. S., Shavlik, D. L., & Touchton, J. G. (eds), *Educating the majority: Women challenge tradition in higher education.* New York: Macmillan Publishing Company.

Bremner, C. S. (1897). *Education of girls and women in Great Britain.* London, UK: Swan Sonnenschein & Co. Inc.

Brown, H. D. (1886). *Two college girls.* Boston: Ticknor and Company.

Bucur, M. (2018). *The century of women: How women have transformed the world since 1900.* New York: Rowman & Littlefield.

Case, C. (1906). *The Masculine in Religion.* Philadelphia: American Baptist Publication Society.

Cassill, R. V. (1961). *Night school.* New York: New American Library.

Champion, T. M. (2006). Title IX: Impact of gender equity on female athletes in intercollegiate athletics (Order No. 3250380). Available from ProQuest Dissertations & Theses Global. (305271762). Retrieved from https://search-proquest-com.contentproxy.phoenix.edu/docview/305271762?accountid=35812

Clarke, E. (1873). *Sex in education: Or a fair chance for girls.* Boston: James R. Osgood and Company.

Clergue, H. (1907). *The salon: A study of French society and personalities in the eighteenth century.* New York: G.P. Putnam's Sons.

Coad, D. (2008). *The metrosexual: Gender, sexuality, and sport.* New York: SUNY Press.

Cooper, J. N. (2013). A culture of collective uplift: The influence of a historically black university/college on black male student athletes' experiences. *Journal of Issues in Intercollegiate Athletics*, 6, 306–331.

Crane, C. (1985). *The western shore.* Salt Lake City, UT: Peregrine Smith Books.

Cuffe, S., Moore, C., & McKeown, R. (2003). ADHD Symptoms in the National Health Interview Survey: Prevalence, Correlates, and Use of Services and Medication. Poster presented at the Fiftieth Anniversary Meeting of the American Academy of Child and Adolescent Psychiatry, Miami, October 20.

Culley, M., & Portuges, C. (eds). (1985). *Gendered subjects: The dynamics of feminist teaching.* London, UK: Routledge & Kegan Paul.

Cunningham, G. (1978). *The new woman and the Victorian novel.* New York: Harper & Row Publishers, Inc.

Dail, P.vW. (2012). *Women and poverty in 21st century America.* Jefferson, NC: McFarland & Company.

Daniels, E. A. (2009). Sex objects, athletes, and sexy athletes: How media representations of women athletes can impact adolescent girls and college women. *Journal of Adolescent Research*, 24(4), 399–422. https://doi.org/10.1177/0743558409336748

David, M. E. (2016). *A feminist manifesto for education.* Cambridge, UK: Polity Press.

Dougherty, C. (2005). Why are Returns to Schooling Higher for Women than for Men? *Journal of Human Resources.* 40:4, pp. 969–88.

Dowhower, A. L. (2000). The experiences of female athletes at a women's college and a coed college (Order No. 9971539). Available from ProQuest Dissertations & Theses Global. (304611319). Retrieved from https://search-proquest-com.contentproxy.phoenix.edu/docview/304611319?accountid=35812

Dupta, N. L. (2000). *Women education through the ages*. New Delhi, India: Concept Publishing Company.

Duquaine-Watson, J. M. (2017). Mothering by degrees: Single mothers and the pursuit of postsecondary education.

Eagan, K., Stolzenberg, E. B., Zimmerman, H. B., Aragon, M. C., Sayson, H. W. & Rios-Aguilar, C. (2017). The American freshman: National norms Fall 2016. Cooperative Institutional Research Program at the Higher Education Research Institute at UCLA.

Eaton, A. A., Saunders, J. F., Jacobson, R. K., & West, K. (2019). Sex Roles: How gender and race stereotypes impact the advancement of scholars in STEM: Professors' biased evaluations of physics and biology post-doctoral candidates. Sex *Roles: A Journal of Research*. Retrieved from https://doi.org/10.1007/s11199–019–01052–w

Eggins, H. (1997). *Women as leaders and managers in higher education*. Bristol, PA: Open University Press.

Eliot, G. (1956). *Middlemarch*. Boston: Houghton Mifflin Company.

Ellis, R. (2014). *The games people play: Theology, religion, and sport*. Eugene, OR: Wipf & Stock.

Ely, R. J., Ibarra, H., & Kolb, D. (2011). Taking gender into account: Theory and design for women's leadership development programs. *The Academy of Management Learning and Education*, 10(3):474–493.

Erskine, S., & Wilson, M. (1999). *Gender issues in international education: Beyond policy and practice*. New York: Falmer Press.

Federal Bureau of Investigation. (2004). Crime in the United Sates, 2003. Washington, D.C.: U.S. Government Printing Office.

Faragher, J. M. (1988). *Women and higher education in American history: Essays from the Mount Holyoke College sesquicentennial symposia*. New York: W.W. Norton & Company.

Farchmin, E. L. (2003). Before the revolution: The experiences of individual women involved in intercollegiate athletics: 1950–1972 (Order No. 3137423). Available from ProQuest Dissertations & Theses Global. (305326975). Retrieved from https://search-proquest-com. contentproxy.phoenix.edu/docview/305326975?accountid=35812

Farrell, A. (2006). Why women don't watch women's sport: A qualitative analysis (Order No. 3217400). Available from ProQuest Dissertations & Theses Global. (305304333). Retrieved from https://search-proquest-com.contentproxy.phoenix.edu/docview/305304333?account id=35812

Farrell, J. T. (1943). *My days of anger*. New York: Vanguard Press.

Farrell, J. T. (1963). *The silence of history*. Garden City, NY: Doubleday and Co.

Fausto-Sterling, A. (1992). *Myths of gender: Biological theories about women and men*. New York: Basic Books.

Female executives say participation in sport helps accelerate leadership and career potential. (2014, Oct 09). PR Newswire Retrieved from https://search-proquest-com.contentproxy. phoenix.edu/docview/1609222124?accountid=35812

Ferguson, M. W. (2003). *Dido's daughters: Literacy, gender, and empire in early modern England and France*. Chicago: The University of Chicago Press.

Fields, S. K. (2008). *Female gladiators: Gender, law, and contact sport in America*. Chicago: University of Illinois Press.

Fischesser, S. M. (2008). "Thanks to title IX": Female athletes' identifications and team sports in transition (Order No. 3323053). Available from ProQuest Dissertations & Theses Global. (304385602). Retrieved from https://search-proquest-com.contentproxy.phoenix.edu/ docview/304385602?accountid=35812

Fischer, S. R. (2003). *A history of reading*. London, UK: Reaktion Books Ltd.

Fonte, M. (2018). *The merits of women: Wherein is revealed their nobility and their superiority to men*. Chicago: University of Chicago Press.

Forman, P. J. (2001). Contesting gender equity: The cooptation of women's intercollegiate athletics (Order No. 3039147). Available from ProQuest Dissertations & Theses Global. (304688416). Retrieved from https://search-proquest-com.contentproxy.phoenix.edu/ docview/304688416?accountid=35812

Fowler, K. J. (2005). *Women who read are dangerous*. New York: Abbeville Press Publishers.

Fox, J. (2019). Girls Have Always Been Better at School. Now It Matters More: The higher-education gender gap has become a major factor in American political and economic life, and it yawns even wider in other rich countries. *Bloomberg Opinion*. Retrieved from https://www.bloomberg.com/opinion/articles/2019-03-06/young-women-widen-the-higher-education-gap

Frankfort, R. (1977). *Collegiate women: Domesticity and career in turn-of-the -century America*. New York: New York University Press.

Freedman, M. B. (1961). Measurement and evaluation of change in college women: final report, August 31, 1961. Mervin B. Freedman, coordinator. Poughkeepsie, NY: Mellon Foundation.

Freire, P. (1970). *Pedagogy of the oppressed*. New York: Continuum Press.

Gallup, Inc. (2016). Understanding life outcomes of former NCAA student-athletes: The Gallup-Purdue index report. Washington, DC: Gallup/NCAA. Retrieved from http://www.ncaa.org/sites/default/files/2016_Gallup_NCAA_StudentAthlete_Report_20160503.pdf

Gawrysiak, E. J., Cooper, J. N., & Hawkins, B. (2013). The impact of baseball participation on the educational experiences of black student–athletes at historically black colleges and universities. *Race Ethnicity and Education*, 1–27. doi:10.1080/13613324.2013.792795].

Gerzema, J., & D'Antonio, M. (2013). *The Athena doctrine*. San Francisco: Jossey-Bass.

Gilbert, B., & Williamson, N. (1974). Women in Sports: A Progress Report. *Sports Illustrated*, 29 July 1974, 28–31.

Gilligan, C. (1993). *In a different voice: psychological theory and women's development*. Cambridge, MA: Harvard University Press.

Glazer-Raymo, J. (2001). *Shattering the myths: Women in academe*. Baltimore: The Johns Hopkins University Press.

Glazer-Raymo, J. (ed). (2008). *Unfinished agendas: New and continuing gender challenges in higher education*. Baltimore: The Johns Hopkins University Press.

Goldin, C., Katz, L., & Kuziemko, I. (2006). The homecoming of American college women: The reversal of the college gender gap. *The Journal of Economic Perspectives*, 20(4), 133–156. Retrieved from http://www.jstor.org/stable/30033687

Gordon, L. D. (1990). *Gender and higher education in the progressive era*. New Haven, CT: Yale University Press.

Gouthro, P., Taber, N., & Brazil, A. (2018). Universities as inclusive learning organizations for women? Considering the role of women in faculty and leadership roles in academe. *The Learning Organization*, 25(1), 29–39. doi:10.1108/TLO-05-2017-0049

Grundy, P., & Shackelford, S. (2005). *Shattering the glass: The remarkable history of women's basketball*. New York: The New Press.

Haines, M. Fertility and Mortality in the United States. EH.Net Encyclopedia, edited by Robert Whaples. March 19, 2008. Retrieved from http://eh.net/encyclopedia/fertility-and-mortality-in-the-united-states/

Hall, O. (1953). *The corpus of Joe Bailey*. New York: Viking Press.

Hanson, S. L., & Kraus, R. S. (1998). Women, sports, and science: Do female athletes have an advantage? *Sociology of Education*, 71(2), 93–110. Retrieved from https://search-proquest-com.contentproxy.phoenix.edu/docview/216487882?accountid=35812

Hanushek, E. A. (2008). Schooling, gender equity, and economic outcomes. In Tembon, M., & Fort, L. (eds), *Girls' education in the 21 st century: Gender equality, empowerment, and economic growth*. Washington, DC: The World Bank.

Harding, S. (1986). *The science question in feminism*. Ithaca, NY: Cornell University Press.

Hawthorne, N. (1828). *Fanshawe*. Boston: Marsh and Capen.

Hesse-Biber, S. N. & Leckenby, D. (2003). *Women in Catholic higher education: Border work, living experiences, and social justice*. New York: Lexington Books.

Higgs, R. J., & Braswell, M. C. (2004). *An unholy alliance: The sacred and modern sports*. Macon, GA: Mercer University Press.

Hinton, D. B. (1994). *Celluloid ivy: Higher education in the movies 1960–1990*. Metuchen, NJ: The Scarecrow Press.

Hoffer, T. B. et al. (2009). Doctorate recipients from US universities: Summary report. Chicago: National Opinion Research Center.

Hoffman, J. L., Rankin, S. R., & Loya, K.I. (2016). Climate as a mediating influence on the perceived academic success of women student-athletes. *Journal for the Study of Sports and Athletes in Education* 10:3, pages 164–184.

Hoffman, J. L., Iverson, S.V., Allan, E. J., & Ropers-Huilman, R. (2010). Title IX policy and intercollegiate athletics: A feminist post structural critique. In Allan, E.J., Iverson, S.V.D & Ropers-Huilman, R. (eds.), *Reconstructing policy in higher education: Feminist post structural perspectives*. New York: Routledge.

Holland, J., Blair, M., & Sheldon, S. (eds). (1995). *Debates and issues in feminist research and pedagogy*. Bristol, PA: Open University.

Horowitz, H. L. (1984). *Alma mater: Design and experience in the women's colleges from their nineteenth-century beginnings to the 1930s*. New York: Alfred A. Knopf.

Hughes, C. D. (2014). *Katharine Drexel: The riches-to-rages tory of an American Catholic saint*. Cambridge, UK: Eerdmans Publishing Co.

Illich, I. (1983). *Deschooling society*. New York: Harper Colophon Books.

Jackovic, T. J. (1999). A comparison of student development outcomes among male revenue athletes, non-revenue athletes, and club sport athletes at an NCAA division I university: A case study (Order No. 9928063). Available from ProQuest Dissertations & Theses Global. (304539039). Retrieved from https://search-proquest-com.contentproxy.phoenix.edu/docview/304539039?accountid=35812

Jacob, B. (2002). Where the boys aren't: Non-Cognitive skills, returns to school and the gender gap in higher education. *Economics of Education Review* 21: 589–598.

Johnson, O. (1968). *Stover at Yale*. New York: Macmillan Company.

Jones, W. A. & Bell, L. F. (2016). Status Report on HBCU Athletics: Participation, Finances, and Student Experiences. Journal for the Study of Sports and Athletes in Education, 48–74. doi:10.1080/19357397.2016.1160694

Katchadourian, H. A. & Boli, J. (1985). *Careerism and intellectualism among college students*. San Francisco: Jossey-Bass.

Kezar, A. J., Carducci, R., & Contreras-McGavin, M. (Eds). (2006). Rethinking the "L" word in higher education. *ASHE Higher Education Report*, Volume 31, Number 6, p 1–218.

King, J. E., & Gomez, G. G. (2008). *On the pathway to the presidency: Characteristics of higher education's senior leadership*. Washington, D.C.: American Council on Education.

Kingfisher, C. (2002). *Western welfare in decline: Globalization and women's poverty*. Philadelphia: University of Pennsylvania Press.

Klevan, S., Weinberg, S. L., & Middleton, J.A. Res High Educ (2016) 57: 223. Retrieved from https://doi.org/10.1007/s11162-015-9384-9

Komarovsky, M. (1985). *Women in college: Shaping new feminine identities*. New York: Basic Books, Inc.

Kramer, J. E. (1981). *The American college novel: An annotated bibliography*. New York: Garland Publishing, Inc.

La Croix, R. M. (2007). "You've come part of the way, baby": The status of women and women's sports in intercollegiate athletics 28 years after title IX (Order No. 3301568). Available from ProQuest Dissertations & Theses Global. (304869300). Retrieved from https://search-proquest-com.contentproxy.phoenix.edu/docview/304869300?accountid=35812

Lang-Peralta, L. (ed). (1999). *Women, revolution, and the novels of the 1790s*. East Lansing: Michigan State Press.

LaVoi, N. M. (ed). (2016). *Women in sports coaching*. London, UK: Routledge.

Leonardi, S. J. (1989). *Dangerous by degrees: Women at Oxford and the Somerville college novelists*. New Brunswick, NJ: Rutgers University Press.

Lindo, J. M., Swensen, I. D. and Waddell, G. R. (2011). Are big-time sports a threat to student achievement? NBER Working Paper No. 17677. Issued in December 2011.

Longino, H. E. & Hammonds, E. "Conflicts and tensions in the feminist study of gender and science." In Holland, J. Blair, M., & Sheldon, S. (eds). (1995). *Debates and issues in feminist research and pedagogy*. Bristol, PA: Open University.

Longman, K. A. & Madsen, S. R. (eds.). (2014). Women & leadership in higher education: Research, theory, and practice. Charlotte, NC: Information Age Publishing, Inc.

Lopez, M. H. & Gonzales-Barrera, A. (2014). Pew Research. March 6. Retrieved from http://www.pewresearch.org/fact-tank/2014/03/06/womens-college-enrollment-gains-leave-men-behind/

Lumina Foundation. (2014). Fact Sheet, November. Washington D.C.: Institute for Women's Policy Research. Retrieved from https://www.luminafoundation.org/files/resources/college-students-raising-children.pdf

Lyons, J. D. (1962). *The college novel in America*. Carbondale: Southern Illinois University Press.

MacNabb, E. L., Cherr, M. J., Popham, S. L. & Prys, R. P. (eds). (2001). *Transforming the disciplines: A women's studies primer*. New York: The Haworth Press.

McCarthy, M. (1963). *The group*. New York: Harcourt, Inc.

Madsen, S. R. (2012). Women and leadership in higher education: Current realities, challenges, and future directions. *Advances in Developing Human Resources*, 14(2), 131–139. Retrieved from https://doi.org/10.1177/1523422311436299.

Malkiel, N. W. (2016). *"Keep the damned women out": The struggle for coeducation*. Princeton, NJ: Princeton University Press.

Manguel, A. (2014). *A history of reading*. New York: Penguin Books.

Marchalonis, S. (1995). *College girls: A century in fiction*. New Brunswick, NJ: Rutgers University Press.

Marcus, J. (2017). Atlantic Monthly. Why Men Are the New College Minority Males are enrolling in higher education at alarmingly low rates, and some colleges are working hard to reverse the trend. August 8. Retrieved from https://www.theatlantic.com/education/archive/2017/08/why-men-are-the-new-college-minority/536103/

Marine, S. B. & Alemán, A. M. M. (2018). Women faculty, professional identity, and generational disposition. *The Review of Higher Education* 41(2), 217–252. Baltimore: Johns Hopkins University Press. Retrieved from Project MUSE database.

Marks, J. (1955). *Life and letters of Mary Emma Woolley*. Washington DC: Public Affairs Press.

Martin, J. & Goodman, J. (2004). *Women and education, 1800–1980*. New York: Palgrave Macmillan.

May, A. M. (2008). *The 'woman question' and higher education: Perspectives on gender and knowledge production in America*. Northhampton, MA: Edward Elgar Publishing.

McClung, L. R. (1996). Negotiation of the gendered ideology of sport: Experiences of women intercollegiate athletes (Order No. 9738061). Available from ProQuest Dissertations & Theses Global. (304308396). Retrieved from https://search-proquest-com.contentproxy.phoenix.edu/docview/304308396?accountid=35812

McKinney, H. D. (2007). The impact of participation in collegiate athletics on women athletes' academic experience at select Jesuit universities (Order No. 3300303). Available from ProQuest Dissertations & Theses Global. (304707313). Retrieved from https://search-proquest-com.contentproxy.phoenix.edu/docview/304707313?accountid=35812

McNeil, M. G. (1985). *History of Mount St. Mary's College, Los Angeles, California 1925–1975*. New York: Vantage Press.

Messner, M. A. & Sabo, D. F. (eds). (1990). *Sport, men, and the gender order: Critical feminist perspectives*. Champaign, IL: Human Kinetics Books.

Miller, J. E. (1997). *Rebel women: Feminism, modernism and the Edwardian novel*. Chicago: University of Chicago Press.

Mitchell, J. S. (1975). *I can be anything: Careers and colleges for young women*. New York: College Entrance Examination Board.

Morgan, C., Bowling, M., Bartram, J., & Kayser, G. L. (2017). Water, sanitation, and hygiene in schools: status and implications of low coverage in Ethiopia, Kenya, Mozambique, Rwanda, Uganda, and Zambia. *International Journal of Hygiene and Environmental Health*, Vol. 220, No. 6, pp. 950–9.

Morley, L. (2014). Lost leaders: women in the global academy. *Higher Education Research and Development*, Vol. 33, No. 1, pp. 114–28.

Morely, L., & Crossouard, B. (2014). Women in higher education leadership in South Asia: Rejection, refusal, reluctance, revisioning. Sussex, UK, University of Sussex, Centre for Higher Education and Equity Research.

Mount Holyoke College. (1937). Alumnae Quarterly. November. South Hadley, MA: Mount Holyoke College.

Mount Holyoke College. (1933). Alumnae Quarterly. November. South Hadley, MA: Mount Holyoke College.

Mount Saint Mary's University. (2019a). Institutional website. Retrieved from https://www. msmu.edu/

Mount Saint Mary's University. (2019b). Intersections: Identity, Access, & Equity. The Report on the Status of Women and Girls in California. Retrieved from https://www.msmu.edu/ media/website/content-assets/msmuedu/home/status-of-women-and-girls-in-california/doc-uments/RSWG-2019-ReportFull.pdf

Mulrine, A. (2001). Are Boys the Weaker Sex? *U.S. News and World Report.* Vol. 131, pp. 40–47.

Murray, B. (2018). A content analysis of sports illustrated's portrayal of female athletes and its impact on society (Order No. 10824220). Available from ProQuest Dissertations & Theses Global. (2072302655). Retrieved from https://search-proquest-com.contentproxy.phoenix.edu/docview/2072302655?accountid=35812

National Endowment for the Arts (NEA). (2002). Reading at risk. Retrieved from https://www.arts.gov/publications/reading-risk-survey-literary-reading-america-0

NCAA. (2016). Revenue and Expenses 2004–2015 Division 1 Intercollegiate Athletics Report. Retrieved from http://www.ncaapublications.com/productdownloads/D1REVEXP2015.pdf

National Center for Educational Statistics (NCES). (2018). Integrated post-secondary educational data system. Retrieved from https://nces.ed.gov/ipeds/

Newcomer, M. (1959). *A century of higher education for American women.* Washington, DC: Zenger Publishing.

Nidiffer, J., & Bashaw, C. T. (eds). (2001). *Women administrators in higher education: Historical and contemporary perspectives.* SUNY Series, Frontiers in Education. Ithaca, NY: State University of New York Press.

Niendorf, K. M. (2007). College women athletes and the life skills they learn from competition (Order No. 3263945). Available from ProQuest Dissertations & Theses Global. (304716688). Retrieved from https://search-proquest-com.contentproxy.phoenix.edu/docview/304716688?accountid=35812

Novak, M. (1994). *The joy of sports: Endzones, bases, baskets, balls, and the consecration of the American spirit.* Lanham, MD: Madison Books.

OECD. (2014). PISA 2012 Results: What Students Know and Can Do (Volume I, Revised edition, February 2014): Student Performance in Mathematics, Reading and Science, PISA. Paris, France: OECD Publishing. Retrieved from http://dx.doi.org/10.1787/9789264208780-en

OECD. (2018). Education at a Glance 2018: OECD Indicators. Paris, France: OECD Publishing. Retrieved from http://dx.doi.org/10.1787/eag-2018-en

OECD and EUPAN. (2015). Diversity and inclusion report. Retrieved from https://www.oecd.org/gov/pem/diversity-and-inclusion.htm

Oliveira, D. F. M., Ma, Y., Woodruff T. K., & Uzzi, B. (2018). Comparison of national institutes of health grant amounts to first-time male and female principal investigators. JAMA. 2019;321(9):898–900. doi:10.1001/jama.2018.21944

O'Meara, K., Kuvaeva, A., Nyunt, G., Waugaman, C., & Jackson, R. (2017). Asked more often: Gender differences in faculty workload in research universities and the work interactions that shape them. *American Educational Research Journal,* 54(6), 1154–1186. Retrieved from https://doi.org/10.3102/0002831217716767

Palmieri, P. A. (1995). *In Adamless Eden: The community of women faculty at Wellesley.* New Haven, CT: Yale University Press.

Patrinos, H. A. (2008). In Tembon, M. & Fort, L. (eds). *Girls' education in the 21st century: Gender equality, empowerment, and economic growth.* Washington, DC: The World Bank.

Pearce, D. (1978). The feminization of poverty: Women, work, and welfare. *Urban and Social Change Review* 11 (1): 28–36.

Pearson, C. S., Shavlik, D. L. & Touchton, J. G. (eds). (1989). *Educating the majority: Women challenge tradition in higher education.* New York: Macmillan Publishing Company.

Pew Research Center. (2016). Book reading 2016. Retrieved from https://www.pewinternet.org/2016/09/01/book-reading-2016/

Pew Research Center. (2019). U.S. women near milestone in the college-educated labor force. Retrieved from https://www.pewresearch.org/fact-tank/2019/06/20/u-s-women-near-milestone-in-the-college-educated-labor-force/

Pope, S. (2017). *The feminization of sports fandom.* New York: Routledge.

Population Research Institute. (2018). Sex-selective abortion. Retrieved from www.pop.org/content/sex-selective-abortion

Potter, D. (2012). *The victor's crown: A history of ancient sport from Homer to Byzantium.* Oxford, UK. Oxford University Press.

Putney, C. (2001). *Muscular Christianity: Manhood and sports in protestant America, 1880–1920.* Cambridge, MA: Harvard University Press.

Quinn, J. (2003). *Powerful subjects: Are women really taking over the university?* London, UK: Trentham Books.

Randleman, M. K. (1997). A study of college and university administrators' attitudes toward athletic competition for women (Order No. 9729154). Available from ProQuest Dissertations & Theses Global. (304445733). Retrieved from https://search-proquest-com.contentproxy.phoenix.edu/docview/304445733?accountid=134061

Ray, R. and Datta, R. 2017. Do separate female toilets in primary and upper primary schools improve female enrollment? A case study from *India. Children and Youth Services Review*, Vol. 79, pp 263–73.

Renn, K. A. (2014). *Women's colleges & universities in a global context.* Baltimore: Johns Hopkins University Press.

Reinert, Leah J. (2016). Silent strategy: Women faculty and the academic profession. University of Minnesota, ProQuest Dissertations Publishing, 10189915.

Rich, A. (1985). Taking women students seriously. In Culley, M. & Portuges, C. (eds), *Gendered subjects: The dynamics of feminist teaching.* London, UK: Routledge & Kegan Paul.

Right to Education Initiative. (2017). Tanzania: Stop threatening rights groups. International organisations urge respect for free expression, association. Retrieved from www.right-to-education.org/news/tanzania-stop-threatening-rights-groups.

Ritter, K. (2012). *To know her own history: Writing at the woman's college, 1943–1963.* Pittsburgh, PA: University of Pittsburgh Press.

Roach, B. L. (2014). It Is Still a Man's Game--Discrimination of Women in Pay and Promotion Forum on Public Policy Online, v2014 n1.

Rogers, A. M. (1938). *Degrees by degrees: The story of the admission of Oxford women students to membership of the university.* Oxford, UK: Oxford University Press.

Ropers-Huilman & Palmer, B. In Allen, J. K., Dean, D. R. & Bracken, S. J. (eds). (2008). *Most college students are women: Implications for teaching, learning, and policy.* Sterling, VA: Stylus.

Ross, S. R. (2005). Challenging the female /athlete paradox: Gender performances of elite women athletes (Order No. 3182368). Available from ProQuest Dissertations & Theses Global. (305004111). Retrieved from https://search-proquest-com.contentproxy.phoenix.edu/docview/305004111?accountid=35812

Rudolph, F. (1990). *The American college and university.* Athens, GA: University of Georgia Press.

Russell, R. S. (2015). What if they were right? title IX and the AIAW's philosophy of coaching and athletic administration (Order No. 10076054). Available from ProQuest Central; ProQuest Dissertations & Theses Global. (1777609488). Retrieved from https://search-proquest-com.contentproxy.phoenix.edu/docview/1777609488?accountid=35812

Rutkoff, P. M. & Scott, W. B. (1986). *New school: A history of the New School for Social Research.* New York: The Free Press.

Sabni, U. (2017). *Reaching for the sky: Empowering girls through education*. Washington, DC: Brookings Institution Press.

Sartorius, K. C. (2014). *Deans of women and the feminist movement: Emily Taylor's activism*. New York: Palgrave Macmillan.

Sax, L. J. (2008). *The gender gap in college: Maximizing the developmental potential of women and men*. San Francisco: Jossey-Bass.

Scholastic. (2019). Kid and family reading report, 7th edition. Retrieved from https://www.scholastic.com/readingreport/home.html

Scripps College. (1931). La Semeuse. Yearbook. Volume One. Claremont, CA: Scripps College.

Scripps College. (nd). Enrollment of Scripps Students at Pomona. Scripps College Archives, Ella Strong Denison Library, Scripps College, Claremont, California.

Scripps College. (1934). Scripps College Aims and Needs, Part II. Scripps College Archives, Ella Strong Denison Library, Scripps College, Claremont, California.

Seiberling, D. (1967). Can Vassar find happiness in New Haven? *Life*. October 13, 1967.

Shavit, Y. & Blossfeld, H. P. (1993). *Persistent inequality: Changing educational attainment in thirteen countries*. Boulder, CO: Westview Press.

Sherry, E., Osborne, A., & Nicholson, M. (2016). Images of sports women: A review. *Sex Roles*, 74(7–8), 299–309. doi:http://dx.doi.org.contentproxy.phoenix.edu/10.1007/s11199-015-0493-x

Sicherman, B. (2010). *Well-read lives: How books inspired a generation of American women*. Chapel Hill, NC: The University of North Carolina Press.

Singh, J. K. S. (2008). Whispers of Change: Female Staff Numbers in Commonwealth Universities. London, Association of Commonwealth Universities.

Solomon, B. M. (1985). *In the company of educated women: A history of women and higher education in America*. New Haven, CT: Yale University Press.

Sommer, M. and Sahin, M. (2013). Overcoming the taboo: advancing the global agenda for menstrual hygiene management for schoolgirls. *American Journal of Public Health*, Vol. 103, No. 9, pp. 1556–9.

Springer, M. (ed.). (1977). *What manner of woman: Essays on English and American life and literature*. New York: New York University Press.

Starr, M. & Brant, M. (1999). It Went Down to the Wire and Thrilled US All, *Newsweek*, 19 July 1999, 50.

Sullivan, A. A. (2019). *Breaking the STEM stereotype: Reaching girls in early childhood*. New York: Rowman & Littlefield.

Tembon, M. & Fort, L. (eds). (2008). *Girls' education in the 21ˢᵗ century: Gender equality, empowerment, and economic growth*. Washington, DC: The World Bank.

The Chronicle of Higher Education. (2018, August 24). DIVERSITY. 64(41), 38+. Retrieved from http://link.galegroup.com.contentproxy.phoenix.edu/apps/doc/A553340708/OVIC?u=uphoenix_uopx&sid=OVIC&xid=fcff5445

The New School. (2014). Institutional website. Retrieved from https://www.newschool.edu/about/history/

The New School. (2019). Strategic Plan. Retrieved from https://www.newschool.edu/about/university-resources/strategic-plan/

Tice, K. W. (2012). *Queens of academe: Beauty pageantry, student bodies, and college life*. Oxford, UK: Oxford University Press.

Tidball, E.M. Women's colleges: Exceptional conditions, not exceptional talent, produce high achievers. In Pearson, C.S., Shavlik, D.L. & Touchton, J.G. (eds). (1989). *Educating the majority: Women challenge tradition in higher education*. New York: Macmillan Publishing Company.

Tidball, E. M., Smith, D. G., Tidball, C. S. & Wolf-Wendel, L. E. (1999). *Taking women seriously: Lessons and legacies for educating the majority*. Phoenix, AZ: American Council on Education, Oryx Press.

Todd, J. (2000). *Mary Wollstonecraft: A revolutionary life*. New York: Columbia University Press.

Toffoletti, K. (2017). *Women sport fans: Identification, participation, representation.* New York: Routledge.

Touchton, J., Shavlik, D., & Davis, L. (1993). *Women in presidencies: A descriptive study of women college and university presidents.* Washington, DC: American Council on Education.

Turpin, A. L. (2016). *A new moral vision: Gender, religion, and the changing purposes of American higher education, 1837–1917.* Ithaca, NY: Cornell University Press.

Umphlett, W. L. (1984). *The movies go to college: Hollywood and the world of the college-life film.* London, UK: Fairleigh Dickinson University Press.

UNESCO. (1992). Role of higher education in promoting education for all. Bangkok, Thailand: UNESCO Principal Regional Office for Asia and the Pacific.

UNESCO. (2018). Global education monitoring report 2018: Gender Review. Paris, France: UNESCO Global Education Monitoring Report team. Retrieved from https://unesdoc.unesco.org/ark:/48223/pf0000261593

UNDP. (2018). Human Development Report. Human Development Indices and Indicators: 2018 Statistical update. Retrieved from, http://report.hdr.undp.org/

United Nations. (1945). Charter of the United Nations. New York, United Nations. (1 UNTS XVI Article1.)

United Nations Statistics Division. The World's Women 2015: Trends and Statistics. Retrieved from https://unstats.un.org/unsd/gender/worldswomen.html

United Nations Population Division. World Population Prospects: 2017 Revision. Retrieved from https://data.worldbank.org/indicator/sp.dyn.tfrt.in.

United Nations, Department of Economic and Social Affairs, Population Division (2017). World Family Planning 2017 - Highlights (ST/ESA/SER.A/414). Retrieved from https://www.un.org/en/development/desa/population/publications/pdf/family/WFP2017_Highlights.pdf

United Nations Educational, Scientific and Cultural Organization (UNESCO), Montreal, the UNESCO Institute for Statistics (UIS) statistics database, last accessed May 2018. Retrieved from https://unstats.un.org/unsd/publications/statistical-yearbook/files/syb61/T06_Gpi_edu.pdf

UN Women. (2017). Facts and Figures: Leadership and Political Participation. New York, United Nations Women. Retrieved from http://www.unwomen.org/en/what-we-do/leadership-and-political-participation/facts-and-figures. (Accessed 5 October 2017.)

Universities Australia. (2017). 2016 Selected Inter-Institutional Gender Equity Statistics. Canberra, Universities Australia.

U.S. Census Bureau. (2000). Retrieved from https://www.census.gov/main/www/cen2000.html.

U.S. Census. (2018). Income and Poverty in the United States: 2017. Retrieved from https://www.census.gov/library/publications/2018/demo/p60–263.html

U.S. Department of Education, National Center for Education Statistics (NCES). (2018). Integrated Postsecondary Education Data System (IPEDS), Spring 2017, Fall Enrollment component; Spring 2017, Human Resources component; and Fall 2016, Completions component. (This table was prepared May 2018.) Retrieved from https://nces.ed.gov/programs/digest/d17/tables/dt17_301.10.asp?current=yes

U.S. Department of Education, National Center for Education Statistics (NCES). (2017). Higher Education General Information Survey (HEGIS), Employees in Institutions of Higher Education, 1970 and 1972, and "Staff Survey" 1976; Projections of Education Statistics to 2000; Integrated Postsecondary Education Data System (IPEDS), "Fall Staff Survey" (IPEDS-S:87–99); IPEDS Winter 2001–02 through Winter 2011–12, Human Resources component, Fall Staff section; IPEDS Spring 2014, Spring 2016, and Spring 2017, Human Resources component, Fall Staff section; and U.S. Equal Employment Opportunity Commission, Higher Education Staff Information Survey (EEO-6), 1977, 1981, and 1983. (This table was prepared December 2017.)

U.S. Department of Education, National Center for Education Statistics. (2018). Digest of Education Statistics, 2016 (NCES 2017–094), Chapter 3.

Verbrugge, M. H. (2012). *Active bodies: A history of women's physical education in twentieth-century America*. New York: Oxford University Press.

Vernos, I. (2013). Research management: quotas are questionable. *Nature*, Vol. 495, No. 7439, p. 39.

Walker, I. M. (1952). *The humanities at Scripps College*. Los Angeles: The Ward Ritchie Press.

Wang, W. (2017, November 7). A Record Share of Men Are "Marrying Up" Educationally. Institute for Family Studies. Retrieved from https://ifstudies.org/blog/a-record-share-of-men-are-marrying-up-educationally

Watt, I. (1957). *The rise of the novel: Studies in Defoe, Richardson and Fielding*. Berkeley: University of California Press.

Webber, K. L. & Rogers, S. M. Res High Educ (2018) Gender Differences in Faculty Member Job Satisfaction: Equity Forestalled? Research in Higher Education. December 2018, Volume 59, Issue 8, pp 1105–1132. Retrieved from https://doi.org/10.1007/s11162-018-9494-2

Weil, D. (1979). *Continuing education*. New York: Ransom, Wade Publishers.

Wheat, C. A., & Hill, L. H. (2016). Leadership identities, styles, and practices of women university administrators and presidents. Research in the Schools, 23(2), 1–16. Retrieved from https://search-proquest-com.contentproxy.phoenix.edu/docview/1881119498?accountid=134061

WHO and UN-Water. (2012). UN-Water Global Analysis and Assessment of Sanitation and Drinking Water (GLAAS) 2012: The Challenge of Extending and Sustaining Services. Geneva, World Health Organization.

Whippoorwill, T. (pseudo.). (1845). *Nelly Brown: Or, the trials, temptations and pleasures of college life*. Boston: "The Yankee Office."

Willard, C. C. (1984). *Christine de Pizan : Her life and works*. New York: Persea Books.

Williams, A. (2017). *The social life of books: Reading together in the eighteenth-century home*. New Haven, CT: Yale University Press.

Wilson, A. S. (2013). A 'saga of power, money, and sex' in women's athletics: A presidents' history of the association for intercollegiate athletics for women (AIAW) (Order No. 3566720). Available from ProQuest Dissertations & Theses Global. (1417073166). Retrieved from https://search-proquest-com.contentproxy.phoenix.edu/docview/1417073166?accountid=35812

Wolfe, A. (2002). *Does education matter? Myths about education and economic growth*. New York: Penguin Books.

Wollstonecraft, M. (2016). *A vindication of the rights of women (1792)*. Sweden: Wisehouse Classics.

Woody, T. (1929). *A history of women's education in the United States*. New York: The Science Press.

Woolf. V. (1929). *A room of one's own*. London, UK: Hogarth Press.

Xavier University of Louisiana. (2019). Institutional website. Retrieved from https://www.xula.edu/

# Index

# About the Author

**Gary A. Berg**, PhD, MFA, is the author/editor of eight previous books, including *Low-Income Students and the Perpetuation of Inequality* and *Lessons from the Edge: For-profit and Nontraditional Higher Education in America*, and numerous academic journal articles, as well as interviews and opinion pieces in popular media. His research has spanned topics such as technology uses for educational purposes, public policy issues on admissions and financial aid, and innovative work in universities and non-profit organizations. Dr. Berg is also a career higher education administrator, including holding the position of dean and associate vice president at California State University Channel Islands for fifteen years.